MW00636760

WANNA TASTE?

Stories and Recipes
from
Mama Carlino's Kitchen

WANNA TASTE?

Stories and Recipes
from
Mama Carlino's Kitchen

Nick Carlino & Angela Carlino Milani
with
Lisa Loeb

Published by
Carlino Enterprises, Inc.

PUBLISHED BY CARLINO ENTERPRISES, INC.
2616 EAST COUNTY LINE ROAD
ARDMORE, PA 19003

Copyright © 2011 by Carlino Enterprises, Inc.

PRINTED IN THE UNITED STATES OF AMERICA
by DavCo Advertising, Inc., Kinzers, Pennsylvania

Library of Congress Catalog Card Number Pending

Cover & Book Design By: Anita W. Taylor

ISBN 13 9780615546988

CONTENTS

In memory of
Angela DiMedio Carlino
1937- 2007

"This book is a collection of my memories and the memories
of others who loved Mama."

~ Nick Carlino

Como Bergamo Udine Laibach Triest Fünfkirchen

Mailand Brescia Vicenza Venedig Fiume Agram Drave

Turin Pavia Verona Padua Polan Karlstadt Novi

Piacenza Parma Mantua Po 35 Zengg Banjaluka

Genua Golf v. Genua Modena Ferrara Ravenna Zara BOSNIEN Saraj

Monaco Spezia Carrara Bologna Rimini Sebenico Spalato Mostar

Ligurisches Florenz S. Marino Ragusa Catt

Meer K. Corso Livorno Ancona 258 1260

Bastia L. Elba Perugia Gr. Sasso 2921 148

Corsica M. Cinto 2710 800 200 **Casoli** M. Gargano Foggia Barletta

Ajaccio Str. v. Bonifacio Civitavecchia Tiber ROM Gaëta Andria Bari

Terranova K. Comino 2717 Neapel Vesuv 1301 Salerno Taranto Brundis

Sassari 1793 M. del Gennargentu 2000 Ischia Capri 3731 Golf v. Taranto

Cagliari 2870 TYRRHENISCHES MEER 3546 3316 Cosenza

2635 MEER Catanzaro K. Rizzuto IONIS

K. Teulada 2000 Liparische I. K. Spartivento 1720

3010 1000 466 Trapani Palermo Messina Reggio

Ägadische I. Alcamo Ätna 3313 Catania 3200

Biserta Marsala Gorgotti Caltagirone Siracusa

Tunis Ras Addar K. Bon (Ital.) Licata Modica Sicilien

Family Tree

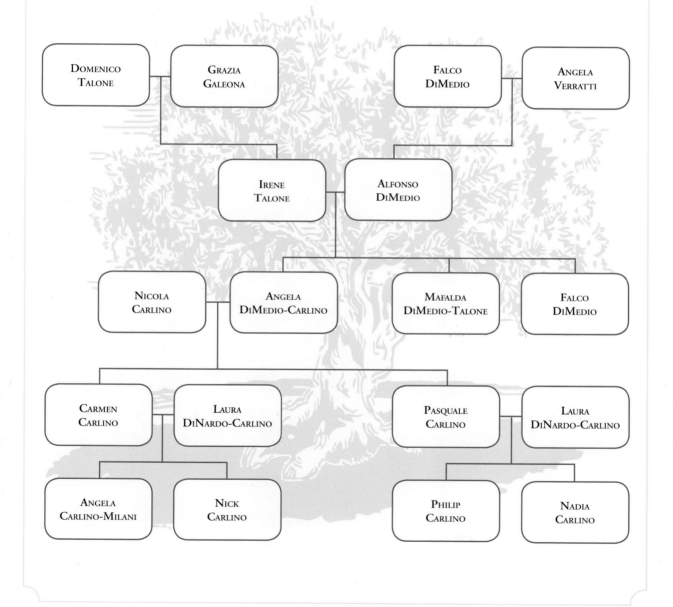

FOREWORD

In honor of Angela DiMedio Carlino

"Love, love, love, that is the soul of genius."
~ Wolfgang Amadeus Mozart

Mama Carlino's family is sharing her story of love and passion. This is her legacy.

Angela Di Medio Carlino was a well-known chef and founder of Carlino's Specialty Foods. *Wanna Taste* is a story of Mama's evolution as well as her family's: one woman dovetailing family and business together into a success. She first offered her old-world recipes in her local neighborhood and later spread them throughout the Philadelphia area. The company has grown from a beginning in her basement kitchen to the present day multi-faceted enterprise, employing over 150 people. The Carlino family members will tell the inside story - no sugar coating.

Some of Mama's favorite recipes will be shared: from rustic to more complex and contemporary dishes with nuances to surprise the tongue.

The stories in the book are from Pat and Laura Carlino, son and daughter-in-law, and from Mama's brother, Uncle Frank, and niece Rosanna. Nick, Angela, Philip, and Nadia Carlino (grandchildren) recall stories from their childhood. Mama's personally trained chefs will also share their stories of Mama.

Many of the conversations were captured as members of the Carlino family worked in the company's two stores.

ACKNOWLEDGMENTS

A giant-sized thank you goes to Dr. Roger C. Loeb, my brilliant brother, for his substantial support and editing. For inspiration, I acknowledge my mother May Bell Loeb, who loved to cook and put up with me begging to lick the beaters. My father James Loeb helped me grow my love of food by sitting me on his lap and sharing tastes directly from "his" plate.

My aunt Etta Sorrentino introduced me to the fine taste of Italian food, mixed with a lot of love.

My sister Wendy read my early writing and patiently helped me. My daughter Laina Loeb Vittone makes my life so much better with her laughing ways.

A number of people encouraged me to go for my dream in writing. They are Sue Brown, Lee Dastur, Jane Kirsch, Julie Ericksen, Pam Komm, John Fattabene, and Joe and E. Tennerelli.

My patient readers are Janice Kullback Wittmershaus, Marcia Closson, Sue Boone, Mary Fallone, Michael Berg, Faeze Woodville, Terry Johnson, and Lisa Tretta Brugger.

A special thanks to the Carlino family. I feel honored to have become acquainted with this creative, enterprising, and energetic family. One by one, members of the Carlino family shared their personal family stories and, just like pearls under soft light, each resonated a glow when talking about their beloved Mama.

It's been a pleasure and joy to know their individual funny bones. I thank you for trusting me with your thoughts, memories, and even tears.

Amongst the banging of pots and pans I've watched chefs unveil their talents in the kitchens. I've watched cakes and pastries finely made, heard about methods of cooking on an open fire, observed grandchildren in motion, and spent countless hours in both Carlino markets viewing the remarkable chefs at their tasks. I've sampled rustic breads, foreign cheeses, and exotic fruit combos.

I have brought home more than I can count: large white Carlino shopping bags, filled with Mama's signature lasagnas, chicken piccata, crostini, mushroom risottos, fig salads, and way too many giant frosting-filled cupcakes. Mama's essence has filtered into my consciousness. She has filled my heart with warmth like a friend from far away and I am grateful.

I salute you - Pat, Laura, Nick, Angela, Philip, Nadia, Uncle Frank, Rosanna, Chef Lou and Chef Jessica, and all the helpers and friends for allowing me this opportunity.

A million thanks.

Lisa Loeb
October 2011

Nick Carlino acknowledges the following people.

Over the last two years ever since the initial stages of this book, I have been fortunate enough to develop a warm, supportive relationship with my co-writer, Lisa Loeb. I would like to thank her for her steadfastness through all of the interviews and revisions, and most importantly, for her dedication to this project. It is impossible to imagine *Wanna Taste* coming to fruition without Lisa's guidance and enthusiasm.

I would like to thank my parents, Pat and Laura Carlino, for always being there to bolster Lisa and me during the difficult times of struggling with the book. I love you and thank you very much!

In addition, I would like to thank my siblings, Angela, Philip, and Nadia for sharing their memories and recipes of Mama with Lisa and me. I love you all so much!

Also, I would like to thank Uncle Frank DiMedio, Zia Maria DiMedio, and Rosanna DiMedio Shayeghi for the tireless hours spent with Lisa and me developing the stories and proofing the recipes and just being there for us when we needed your assistance. I cannot thank you enough!

Lastly, I would like to thank Chef Jessica Perez, Chef Alejandro Perez, Chef Lou Pietrantonio, John DiMichele, Kathy DiMichele, Bruce Mowday, Emmy Shea, and Julian Kornacki. I couldn't have done it without your love and support.

Nick Carlino
October 2011

Introduction

The Project Begins:

Preparing my table at a local health fair, I somehow sensed great energy streaming from the next booth. The sign over the booth said, "Carlino's Market." Glancing over, I saw a young man busily transforming his space with exotic fresh flowers and intriguing little samples of foodstuffs. He caught my admiring glance, and said, "Hi, I'm Nick Carlino. Would you like to taste a sample of our edamame salad?" Of course I did. The salad tasted of just-picked-from-the-garden freshness. It was highlighted with bits of peppers, parsley, and wheat berries that jolted my taste buds. I told Nick, "YUM! This is incredible! Lightly spiced, totally delicious."

I continued to nibble at my salad as Nick introduced himself as Mama Carlino's grandson. He was tall and slender with dark eyes. Everything about Nick said enthusiasm. During that memorable day I watched him attend to every detail, ensuring that everything looked and tasted just so. He was friendly and easygoing. We struck up a casual acquaintance. Soon we were sharing our life plans and passions. I had recently returned from my long-delayed visit to Tuscany and Umbria in Italy and was preparing an article for the travel section of the *Philadelphia Inquirer*. Nick volunteered that he had a heart-felt wish to honor his grandmother's memory with a book about her cooking and background in Casoli, Italy. The family store in Ardmore was well known to me. I was saddened to hear of the sudden passing of Mama Carlino when Nick told me.

Nick recalled how life changed in a heartbeat on November 4, 2007. "I was in a college accounting class when my grandmother suddenly took ill. I felt my phone vibrate and saw my mom's name, I knew something was wrong. I left the classroom and found out my grandmother was in Bryn Mawr Hospital. In those first 30 seconds my heart dropped, I couldn't breathe, and I knew a critical person in my life might not be around for me much longer.

"Once I regained control of my emotions, I frantically drove to the hospital and found Mama, my best friend, lying on a hospital bed only able to use the left side of her body due to a massive stroke. Even with only half her body able to move, Mama's heart monitor skyrocketed when she heard my voice. When I ventured closer to her, she used her good arm to pull me close to her chest. She was unable to speak but it did not matter for I knew what she was saying. She loved me and did not want to leave, but she had to. She knew her earthly destiny was complete and now the time had come to spend eternal life with the rest of her family.

"As much as I did not want my best friend to leave my life, I realized she needed to be at peace and I knew her presence would stay with me always."

Throughout the day at the health fair Nick sent to me plate after plate laden with succulent morsels. I had become a fish and I couldn't resist the bait. I had to know more. Nick told me that his duties managing Carlino's kept him extremely busy but the tribute to his grandmother dominated his thoughts. Hmmm, I wondered if I could help.

Perhaps our paths were destined to cross that day. My grandfather Harold Loeb had been a writer and editor in the 1920's and 30's. He published a small literary magazine called Broom which featured works of acclaimed expatriate authors and painters of the era.

The day I met Nick I began sketching the outlines of a memoir brimming with photos and recipes – a fitting tribute to Mama Carlino.

Mama's wooden stool

CHAPTER ONE

THE CARLINOS

Carlino's Specialty Foods and Catering is an astonishingly successful gourmet food company in the towns of Ardmore and West Chester, Pa. The company was founded and nurtured lovingly by a spunky and enthusiastic Italian woman known locally as Mama Carlino.

Mama was from Abruzzo, Italy. Her business was located in an old house in Ardmore where modest, single-family and twin houses sit tidily side by side. There are a few other buildings devoted to businesses, but it's a surprise to come upon the flurry of activity that surrounds the Italian market known as Carlino's.

During summer months passersby can't help but notice the tomato plants, heavy with ripe fruit, climbing up poles in the parking lot. Fresh tomatoes mean fresh ingredients, a small clue to the dedication and care which have led to Carlino's terrific success. Inside the store, the rich aroma of chicken soup pervades the room. Gilda, a long-time friend of the family, stands at a small table ladling out soup from an ancient black iron pot. She smiles graciously and hands out paper cups filled with steaming, flavorful broth.

Shoppers navigate their way through the narrow aisles. The market is a pageant of fine foods, fresh bright produce, and exquisite desserts. There are large moist figs lying heaped in a woven basket. Shelves hold a wide assortment of imported goods. Vegetables and fruits are displayed in even rows exploding with freshness in colors of red, yellow, and purple. On a large table a huge assortment of cheeses is stacked, Locatelli and Parmigiano Reggiano along with lesser-known brands. Cashiers chat amicably with customers near the door.

Mama's empty stool still sits behind a counter where she used to sit and greet customers. Norman, a manager, has chosen to leave it standing as a silent tribute to Mama. Mama's chef's apron and utensils are framed and hanging on the wall. Tantalizing, smoky aroma leads one to the back of the store where the flaming brick ovens work continuously, birthing yummy crusted breads. A hum of energy creates a lively ambience.

A customer from the take-out section raves about the Caesar salad, "It's like no other! There are large herby croutons…and the dressing is tangy yet sits lightly on the lettuce." Another long-time customer Lori Faust is here on a nostalgic shopping trip. She says, "My grandmother made meatballs and freetes (fried dough) just like Mama Carlino." Lori is representative of hundreds of customers for whom tradition is an essential part of life. Carlino's recipes have traveled across oceans and generations. Connectedness to the past and to a heritage is what the Carlino family is all about.

Mama's family

Pat Carlino is Mama's son and business partner. He remembers growing up with a woman whose passions for food were unlimited. "When I was nine, Mama taught me the importance of getting the right ingredients from the right sources," he explains. "In our neighborhood I knew Sandi's Market had the best flour. The Head Nut was the place for buying anise and spice. Lipmans Market was the favorite for overall shopping. All of these stores were local, within the radius of about a mile. I learned about pricing by doing most of the buying and adding everything up. I figured out she was not charging enough!"

From the beginning family and community members provided mutual support. "When we first opened our doors, the Lipmans were the first ones to come into the store and give us their blessings."

This tradition of working together continued through the years to shape Carlino's success.

"When I was old enough to drive," Pat continues, "we drove to Jersey and New York – observing, taking notes, being constantly on the uptake for creative ideas to add to our knowledge of the food business." When sales increased, Pat developed the drive for retail business. Pat says, "We made a good team, my early experiences turned out to be a great education in building relationships. When it was time to pick a location for the market Mama thought our small street on County Line Road was the center of consumerism. Pat chuckles, "Mama was adamant! Besides we could walk to work!"

Nicola Carlino was Mama's husband for 52 years. Nicola was an old-school Italian, raised in a strict, religious household. He and Mama were matched with similar strengths: perfectionism in regards to food, a strong work ethic, and a never-ending drive. Both had strong opinions. It was inevitable that the two would struggle at times.

In the early days of the business Nicola oversaw the sauce and pasta making. He and Carmen went back to Italy to purchase the pasta and tortellini machines. In addition, he and Mama had years of experience in wine making. He took special pride in continuing to make homemade wines. Mama often used them in her recipes for unique nuances.

Carmen Carlino was Mama's oldest son and Pat's much-loved brother. He brought his considerable talents to the team. Although his life was short he will be remembered for his drive and ability to push through the hard times and enjoy the good times.

Laura DiNardo Carlino is Mama's daughter-in-law. Laura is the "big cheese" who keeps everything in line. She oversees the family home, the kids' schedules, and her job. "When you have a family business like ours, it's always something," she says with a hint of fatigue. "Computers on the blip, phone systems needing replacement, or freezers quitting. Everything must be handled in a timely fashion."

Yet she appears in fine spirits as she balances all these spinning plates, with hardly a ruffle to her well-groomed hair.

Laura has been an integral part of the team since she began working for Mama at age 18. She explains, "The Carlinos and the DiNardos knew each other from the old country. We immigrated from the same part of Italy, Abruzzo. In the United States our family often visited Mama when she was selling cookies from her basement in Ardmore. As I grew older, she noticed me and was very motherly. I think she had her eye on me for one of her sons!"

Nick Carlino is Mama's grandson and "marketing magnate" for Carlino's. Mama's influence is apparent throughout her lineage. Her expansive reach particularly touches grandson Nick. "Nicky," she would say, "You must have passion for anything you do in life. And everything you do must come from the heart!"

"Mama taught me to be who I am," he confides. "She taught me how to be respectful and how to interact with all kinds of people. She taught me the art of salesmanship. I'd watch her behind the counter asking, 'Wanna taste?'"

Nick's face is a river of rapidly shifting currents, serious pride, passionate commitment, and a quirky sense of humor. A recent graduate of St. Joseph's University in food marketing, Nick uses his formal training as well as his life experiences to seek out inventive ideas for expanding the business. Carlino's Specialty Foods is clearly at the center of his life.

Angela Carlino Milani is Mama's granddaughter, a chef and cooking instructor. Angela, Mama's namesake, has strong memories of her grandmother. "When I was a young child," she remembers fondly, "the kitchen in Mama's house just pulled me in. I experienced a world flowing with smells and tastings. Being at Mama's side, I was in the middle of the action: pans clanging, Mama directing, and her hands creating. I loved helping her mix herbs and prepare dishes for the evening meals.

"Fun in the kitchen every day, that's what I carry with me. When I went to chef school I felt proud. Mama didn't have the chance to go to chef school. She would like knowing her traditions will go forward."

"I try to recreate this with children in my cooking classes. They come in ready to have fun, just like I did when I was a girl by Mama's side. My aim is to engage young minds and also teach where food comes from and how to feed the body well. As Mama would say, 'You gotta have fun!'"

Nick and Angela Carlino both remember the wisdom and love that Mama expressed every day to each of them and to all of their customers as well.

This book is a conduit for her stories and some of her special recipes for customers as well as foodies unfamiliar with Carlino's.

The story begins in 1983 when Mama opened the tiny storefront in suburban Philadelphia. At that time it was difficult to find homemade pasta in southeastern Pennsylvania. When the local folks first tasted Mama Carlino's cookies and homemade pasta and pastries, the word quickly flew. Mama had brought the best flavors of Italy to Ardmore.

CHAPTER TWO

THE DIMEDIO FAMILY HISTORY
— WAR YEARS —

Mama, the mover and shaker of the family, entered the world on November 4, 1937, in Casoli, Italy. Her parents Alfonzo DiMedio, 28, and Irena, 17, were married in Casoli in 1933. Irena gave birth to three children. Angela (Mama Carlino) was first born and following her was another girl, Mafalda. Brother Falco, known as Uncle Frank, was then born. The three children lived with their parents, grandparents, and an aunt and her child on a small farm in Casoli.

Frank recalls his other sister Malfalda as a frail child. She stayed in Italy and after high school studied to become a seamstress. Her skills were exceptional as she made wedding gowns and eventually worked for a company selling sewing machines and teaching people how to use them. Rosanna, Mama's niece, recalls, "Over the years everyone went back to visit with Malfalda." Although Mama's parents immigrated to the United States, they returned to Italy in 1987 and lived with Mafalda until they died. Mafalda's son Lello and his family live in the same house as his mother.

The DiMedio children were born into years of strife. The war years (1940-45) which occurred when they were small, took a terrible toll on Italy. Nearly four million Italians served in the military during World War II and nearly half a million Italians, including numerous civilians, died. Though the DiMedio's farm had once been self-sufficient, it, like the rest of Italy, suffered egregiously. Mama's father was forced to enlist in the army.

Hungry German soldiers ravaged the countryside of everything of value, stripping the fields of foodstuffs. Insecurity and fear of German brutality were constant companions. Rumors passed from family to family about neighbors who had been shot.

Italy, under the leadership of Mussolini, had overextended its meager resources. Poorly equipped and badly funded, the Italian military had overreached. In 1940, at Hitler's behest, Italy signed the Pact of Steel tying their fortunes to Germany. By 1941,

Mama's parents, Irena and Alfonso,
after they emigrated from Italy

Alfonso and Irena, circa 1990

Nonna Grazia and Nonno Domenico

Nicola and Carmen and a cousin
on the Carlino steer

Italy was totally dependent on Germany. There was to be no active military forays until 1943. Italy could not afford the missions, but Hitler would not wait. Italy became impoverished.

Uncle Frank recalls how once the Italians had capitulated to the Allies, food was scarce and neighbors called upon neighbors to help. It's highly probable that this experience is one reason Mama bonded so tightly with her family, she never wanted to lose them.

The day came when a pair of German soldiers forced their way into the DiMedio home. While the children cowered in terrified silence, the soldiers interrogated and strip-searched the adults. Over and over the soldiers yelled, "Where is father?" Mama's mother Irena tried to explain but the language barrier made it difficult. They accused her of hiding him. One soldier even searched the barn futilely. The family did not even know where he was, as letters came only infrequently. Finally, they demanded the one chicken in the yard, and forced Irena to kill it and cook it for them.

It was no longer safe for the DiMedios to stay on the farm. Before leaving, they gathered grain and a few other items, and hid them in the barn under hay bales. Uncle Frank recalls being hoisted into a basket, slung over the donkey's back, his young cousin deposited in the other side. The family traveled to a safe zone where they were housed with hundreds of others in a large barn-like structure. They stayed approximately three months before a cousin got paperwork and escorted them back home.

Returning home the family discovered their precious few pieces of jewelry had been stolen, but the grain they had hidden in the barn was safe, enabling the family to eat. Again neighbors cooperated with each other and traded goods.

Uncle Frank, just a boy when his father returned, has one vague memory. He said, "Father wore some baggy type socks!"

This harsh family history did not leave Mama's memory, and she would tell Pat over the years, "Don't bury me without some money, I don't want to be poor." On the day of Mama's funeral, Pat remembered his mother's wishes, and went to the bank and withdrew four new ten dollar bills, one for each grandchild. Mama was dressed in a beautiful gold gown, the cherished dress she had worn to celebrate her 50th wedding anniversary. She was laying so peacefully that she looked as if she had just fallen asleep on the chaise lounge on the back patio. Pat gently placed the four ten dollar bills in her handbag, by her side.

Mama Carlino, circa 1972

Le Totere Casolane

(Cream-filled Pastry Cones indigenous to Casoli, Abruzzo, Italy)

Yield: 10 | Time: 45 minutes

FOR THE DOUGH

INGREDIENTS:

1 egg
2 tablespoons sugar
1 tablespoon vegetable oil
¼ teaspoon pure vanilla extract
⅛ teaspoon baking powder
1 cup all purpose flour

4 cups vegetable oil, for deep frying
5 cups Crema Pasticcera,
 (recipe on page 149)
10 metal pastry cones
 (found in specialty kitchen store)

DIRECTIONS:

1. Beat egg with sugar in a large mixing bowl with a fork.

2. Add oil and vanilla. Continue beating.

3. Slowly add baking powder and ¾ cup flour.

4. Sprinkle flour over work surface. Turn dough onto work surface.

5. Knead dough by hand until ball of dough bounces back when finger is pressed into the dough.

6. Meanwhile, heat oil in a heavy-bottomed pot with sides 4-6 inches high.

7. Submerge one metal cone in hot oil until cone is hot.
   *This step is to grease the outside of the cone.

8. Repeat Step 7 until all 10 metal cones are greased.

9. Sprinkle work surface with flour. Roll out dough with rolling pin until the dough reaches approximately 15 inches in width and rolls out very thin.

10. Cut 1 inch wide strips from the dough using a pastry wheel or a sharp knife.

11. Wrap 1 strip around 1 greased cone overlapping edges starting at the widest end. Pinch point of cone so that dough does not unravel when fried.

12. Carefully place wrapped cone into hot oil until golden brown.

13. Let cool slightly (until cool enough to handle). Remove metal cone insert as quickly as possible as to not allow cold dough to stick to the metal and rip.

14. Place cone on a paper towel lined platter.

15. Repeat Steps 11-14 until all dough is fried.

16. Allow cones to cool completely before filling.

17. Fill cones with Crema Pasticcera with a small spoon or pipe into cone with a piping bag.

18. Refrigerate filled cones overnight before serving.

Store unfilled, fried cone shells by placing them in an air-tight container. The shells will last two days in refrigeration and 1 month in the freezer.

Zia Maria DiMedio, Uncle Frank's wife; who was always Mama's assistant when making the "totere" for any family function.

Chapter Three

All About Mama

Uncle Frank refers to his sister by a variety of names, Angie, Angelina, Angela, but which ever name is used, she was the queen bee of the Carlino family and business. The business is fueled by passion for authentic dishes, using old world techniques creating a link back to the family origins in Casoli, Italy. Three generations of Carlinos have not lost touch with their history and they pay homage by continuing to make the traditional foods.

Each member of the family has drive, high energy, and a strong work ethic. Mama's grandchildren definitely have the genes. Even youngest granddaughter Nadia knows what she wants for the future exclaiming, "Mama taught me exactly what to do in the kitchen and someday I'm going to be a main chef!"

Rosanna, Mama's niece, describes Mama's methods, "If my aunt wanted something, like a certain piece of clothing, we'd go to countless stores before she found exactly what she was looking for. It's the same with her cooking, the drive for perfection."

Mama Carlino was always perfectly coiffed, dressed in a spotless white chef jacket with earrings in place and hair impeccably fashioned. Grandson Nick recalls her preference for V-neck blouses and describes his grandmother's appearance, as stylish. Nick quotes her as saying, "When you leave the house, look your best and have 20 bucks in your pocket. You never know!" Noted for her smooth youthful skin, she also had an enormous smile when she chose to display it. Nadia calls her grandmother a fashionista!

In a home video Mama is holding a beautiful loaf of fresh bread. One can see the love and care present in her eyes when she looks at her son Pat and the way she pecks the cheek of her grandson Nick.

Nick and his mother agree. Nick said, "Mama's success was due in part to her nature, her authenticity. When she'd share a prayer card or offer advice, people knew that she wished only the best for them. Her caring always came through." This was true in business, with her family, and in the community at large.

The Carlino house built in 1962

Casoli - Viale Francesco Paolo Michetti

Mama always envisioned the future, wanting to make sure her traditions continued and the business continued to grow. Pat remembers her talking about a book and the importance of getting the recipes recorded. "It was a goal she talked about frequently," he says. "In her later years she'd say, 'Angela and Nick will write the book of my recipes.'"

Casoli

Taking a step back, let's visit young Angela in the tiny town of Casoli. Mama's brother Uncle Frank recalls that Angela had two favorite places on the farm. One was in the kitchen where the smells of baking hung sweet, mixing with the smell of an open fire. The other was the loamy fields where she ran barefoot and helped harvest ripe vegetables and other produce. As the oldest child she often helped her mother by going with her to the community fountain to draw water for washing the clothes.

At age three, dressed in a long styled skirt and a simple blouse, Angela pulled herself up to the table. Standing on a little wooden stool, she watched as flour flew and dough tumbled. As the eldest of three siblings she was expected to learn to cook. The family's farm was located in Casoli, known as a town with a soul in the Abruzzo region of Italy.

Farming the earth was grinding labor but the culture Mama grew up with was rich in traditions. Cooking had to be inventive; using what was available at the time. Uncle Frank recalls the two staples were handmade cheese and sausage. "We dried the cheese in the kitchen, then stored it in oil," he recalled.

A traditional dish made by the DiMedio family was pasta fagioli, Uncle Frank recalled. He said,

"We made fagioli by using our own white beans, harvested in the fall, dried in winter. We'd boil a huge pot of water over the fire. We would boil the beans and keep adding water during the day. We'd put flour on the big table, make a well, add a little salt and water, and massage it. Then the dough would be rolled and flattened to a quarter inch thick. Tomato sauce was poured on the top followed by the beans. To make it a little spicier we add a little pepperoncini." A mix of goat and cow cheese was grated on top of the dish.

Chuckling, Frank recalled, "On the farm I had to milk the sheep. They did not like to be milked. Oh, those sheep were stubborn!"

With no refrigeration Laura described the cooling method on the farm. She said, "The well was used to chill items for the day like wine, fruit, or watermelon. Everything was pickled or cured to preserve it as there was no refrigeration."

Uncle Frank's favorite dish is polenta. Uncle Frank's jolly demeanor soars when he talks about food. His wiry eyebrows move up and down and his thick hands fold into shapes as he recalls the days when he was young. "My grandmother would make sausage and peppers to go on top of the polenta. She'd spread the polenta out on the table and I'd take my fork and mark where my section would begin, right by a big juicy sausage."

The DiMedio children: Angela,
Falco (Uncle Frank), and Mafalda

Polenta su Tavola di Legno

(Polenta on a Wooden Board)

~ Serves: 6-8 | Time: 1 hour ~

INGREDIENTS:

2 liters water
1 ½ teaspoons kosher salt
1 pound yellow cornmeal

6 tablespoons Extra Virgin Olive Oil
Homemade Bolognese Sauce
(recipe on page 39)

DIRECTIONS:

1. In an extra-large, heavy-bottomed pot, bring water and salt to a boil.

2. Add cornmeal, ½ cup at a time, stirring constantly with whisk to prevent lumps.

3. Cook over medium heat, stirring constantly, until the polenta is very thick and has the consistency of thick mashed potatoes, 30 to 45 minutes.

   When the polenta begins to stiffen be sure to start using a wooden spoon for the rest of the cooking process.

4. Add the olive oil in a steady stream while stirring to give the polenta a silky texture and sheen.

5. Pour and spread polenta onto a long wooden board (ideally 2' x 3').

6. Top with homemade Bolognese Sauce and enjoy!

The pouring of the polenta!

Pizze e Foie

(Cornmeal "Pizza" & Greens)

∽ Serves: 8 | Time: 1 hour ∽

INGREDIENTS:

4 heads wild chicory or escarole;
  using only the outer green leaves
3 heads Swiss chard
1 head cabbage, preferably Savoy
¾ cup extra virgin olive oil
½ pound Pancetta, diced
3 cloves of garlic
½ red pepper, medium dice
Hot pepper flakes, to taste
Pizza di Granturca (Cornmeal "Pizza"),
  (recipe on page 18)

DIRECTIONS:

1. Bring a large pot of water to a boil.

2. Wash greens well and coarsely chop.

3. Add greens to pot of boiling water and cook slowly for 15 minutes.

4. Drain greens completely using a colander and set aside.

5. In a large fry pan, fry the pancetta, garlic and red pepper in the olive oil. Season with salt and add the hot pepper flakes.

6. Add the drained greens slowly to frying pan and mix well together.

7. Break up the pizza with your hands and incorporate into the greens. Serve warm.

Pizza di Granturca

(Cornmeal "Pizza")

INGREDIENTS:

1 pound cornmeal (polenta flour)
1 tablespoon salt
1 cup boiling water
2 tablespoons Extra Virgin Olive Oil

DIRECTIONS:

1. Preheat oven to 350°F.

2. On a work surface, make a well with the cornmeal and add salt.

3. Slowly add the boiling water, using a fork, and bring flour and water together until it forms a soft ball.

   **USE CAUTION WITH THIS STEP. BE MINDFUL WHEN POURING AND STIRRING THE BOILING WATER AS TO NOT SCORCH YOUR HAND.

4. Oil a baking dish with olive oil; and flatten the dough to about 1 inch thickness.

5. Bake for approximately 25 minutes or until a toothpick inserted into the center comes out clean.

6. Let cool for about 10 minutes.

7. Break apart into chunks and add to Pizza e Foie recipe.

This recipe is truly Abruzzese. Mama grew up eating this dish because everyone grew their own greens, and cornmeal was readily available. Mama would always tell the children stories of her childhood and how this hearty dish was truly a "healthy food" before eating healthy food became a fad.

The Carlino and DiMedio families, circa 1972

IMMIGRATION

The first of the Carlino family to emigrate in 1921 was Pasquale, Pat's namesake, with others following. Philip, an uncle and American citizen, was able to sponsor the family and in 1968 Angela, then 31, Nicola, and the two children entered the United States by way of New York City.

Upon arrival, Uncle Philip and Uncle Frank drove to the port to pick up the family. It was a time of great excitement and Uncle Frank recalls how he drove his Pontiac GTO. Carmen, eleven years old and full of high spirits, begged to sit in the front beside Uncle Frank as his family was about to zoom off into a new life.

The family lived at Philip's home on Penn Street in Bryn Mawr, Pennsylvania, for six months before moving to Ardmore. The family adjusted quickly as Carmen received extra help from a nearby school and six-year-old Pat assimilated easily.

Once in their own home Angela's busy hands were soon creating delectable biscotti in the basement of the small house. Pat, Mama's son, reaches back into his memories and sees his mother, apron clad and hair neatly combed, cooking in the kitchen. He remembers being sent out for fresh supplies in order to keep up the pace necessary for the increasing demand. He says, "Her mind hummed with ideas for innovation, she tested and tasted her way to new dishes, often rising in the middle of the night to try something new."

Basic Risotto

~ Yields: 2 cups ~

INGREDIENTS:

2 cups low-sodium chicken broth
3 tablespoons unsalted butter, at room
    temperature
½ small onion, chopped
¾ cup Arborio rice
¼ cup dry white wine
¼ cup finely grated Parmigiano
    Reggiano Cheese
¼ teaspoon kosher salt
¼ teaspoon freshly ground black pepper

DIRECTIONS:

1. In a medium saucepan, bring the broth to a simmer over high heat. Reduce the
   heat to low and keep the broth hot.

2. In a large, heavy saucepan, melt 2 tablespoons of the butter over medium heat.
   Add the onion and cook, stirring frequently until tender, about 3 minutes. Add
   the rice and stir to coat with the butter.

3. Add the wine and simmer until most of the liquid has evaporated, about 1
   minute. Add ½ cup hot broth and stir until almost completely absorbed, about 2
   minutes.

4. Continue cooking the rice, adding the broth, ½ cup at a time, stirring constantly
   and allowing each addition of broth to absorb before adding the next.

5. Cook the rice until tender but still firm to the bite and the mixture is creamy,
   about 20 minutes.

6. Remove the pan from the heat and stir in the remaining butter, Parmigiano
   Reggiano Cheese, salt, and pepper.

Pasta e Fagioli

(Pasta & White Bean Soup)

❧ Serves: 4-6 | Time: 30 minutes ❧

INGREDIENTS:

1 small onion, peeled and chopped finely
4 tablespoons Extra Virgin Olive Oil
4 garlic cloves, peeled and minced
3 cups canned Italian tomato puree
   (preferably San Marzano tomatoes)
8-10 fresh basil leaves, cut julienne (fine ribbons)
Handful chopped Italian flat leaf parsley
3 (15-ounce) cans Italian cannellini beans, undrained,
   or cooked dried white beans with their cooking liquid
5 cups water
Salt and freshly ground black pepper, to taste
4 ounces tubetti pasta

DIRECTIONS:

1. In a medium size soup pot sauté the onion with olive oil until soft and translucent. Add the garlic and sauté until lightly golden.

2. Add the tomatoes, basil, and parsley. Cook over moderately high heat until tomatoes release their natural juices.

3. Add the beans with their liquid and the 5 cups water. Cook over medium heat for at least 15 minutes or until beans begin to break down and soup thickens.

4. Add the pasta to the simmering soup and cook until al dente. Season with salt and pepper. Serve immediately.

For a more rustic pasta e fagioli sauté ¼ pound diced pancetta with the onion in Step 1, and continue the recipe from this point.

Pasta e Fagioli

Nicola and Angela posing on the day the Church blessed their union

Chapter Four
Mama and Nicola

"Young love sometimes can't wait!" Laura Carlino says in her knowing way.

On August 6, 1955, defying their parents, Angela DiMedio, 17, and Nicola Carlino, 23, eloped. The two traveled to the Carlino farm in Casoli and hid in Nicola's room. Angela DiMedio and her sister Mafalda both eloped at tender ages. A story brews behind the facts. Stridently, Laura Carlino shares her version of the story. She said, "Young Angela had a romantic vision. The decision was made very quickly with a little assistance from her sister Mafalda who was two years younger."

Pat describes how the couple met. "Angela and Nicola only caught glimpses of each other when they happened to be in town at the same time. They didn't really know each other, for in those days teens were strictly supervised. They were allowed to attend dances as long as parents were nearby, ever watchful. No inappropriate behavior would be tolerated!"

After noticing Angela in town, Nicola wanted to let Angela know his feelings so he devised a plan, literally up his sleeve. He knew the only way to meet her was to attend a dance. Dances were held periodically at parents' homes. A man with a plan gets there early. Nicola, dressed in his best clothes with his hair combed neatly back off his forehead, waited for Angela to arrive. As the romantic music began to play the couples paired off, surrounded by darkness. Nicola approached Angela and asked her to dance. As she placed her hand in his, she noticed his enigmatic smile and his muscled shoulders and then she felt something in her hand. Daring to look, she realized it was Caramella (candy) slipped there by Nicola.

While they danced in and around the other couples, Angela felt flutters of excitement; she thought, "He is brave!" As Nicola moved her around with speed, she also worried; what if the candy slips and falls? If discovered it would be considered an indiscretion and punishment would follow. After finishing the dance, Angela ran off to scout out her sister; she wanted to share a secret: she liked Nicola Carlino!

Mafalda had her own agenda. She and her own secret beau wanted to marry as quickly as possible. Angela, being the oldest, needed to marry first as was the rule of the time. When Mafalda heard of the attraction between Angela and Nicola, she quickly told her sister, "It's simple. I'll help you." Angela agreed. Putting their heads together they concocted a plan, an elopement would allow them to marry.

The day was set and the plan hatched. Nicola and Angela ran through the countryside hand in hand until they reached Nicola's farm and snuck in while the family was out in the fields. They made it up the stairs and into his room without being seen. With a sigh of relief they locked the door. Happiness lifted their young spirits as they congratulated each other on pulling off a coup. Grinning at each other they exalted and fell into each other's arms. But fear also gripped them as Nicola's Uncle Pasquale did not approve of the match. He had a harsh way about him and he had a shotgun. Rumor had it that he was ready to shoot them both!

For the wedding dinner that night, one of Nicola's cousins gathered some food and hoisted it up to the bedroom by way of pulley. The couple's dinner was simple fare, comprised of only three foods: rigatoni, two pieces of lamb, and a slice of watermelon." Out of fear and embarrassment the young couple stayed in the room for two days.

Once the couple had been together for the night they had to be married. They proceeded to the village church and asked the priest to perform the marriage. He refused to marry them at the altar but instead took them to the back of the church and performed the marriage there. Papers were signed and the deed was done. Angela's brother Uncle Frank recalls how quickly his family changed. "Both sisters eloped, one after the other! Grazie a Dio!"

Their union could not be undone. When Nicola and Angela sheepishly came out of the room they went directly to the fields and didn't say a word to anyone, so naughty they felt. In August all was forgiven as every person was needed to harvest the crops.

After two years of marriage Angela discovered she was expecting a baby. The couple, as is the custom, hoped for a baby boy. The pregnancy was uneventful, but Nicola and Uncle Frank will never forget the difficult day of the birth.

At that time, summoning a doctor required riding a horse about five miles. When Angela went into labor, a midwife was called to assist. Uncle Frank and Nicola waited outside and paced back and forth as the birthing process inched along. Hours passed in heavy labor but the child did not emerge. Mama Mia! It was a difficult birth. The two men worried as they heard screams reverberate over and over, scorching their ears. Angela's mother Irena and grandmother Grazia both were in attendance. The strain took a toll on all of them.

The couple celebrating their "honeymoon" in the wheat fields

As it turned out the baby boy, to be named Carmen, was huge, more than ten pounds. The doctor arrived shortly after the birth. Apparently Mama had hemorrhaged. It was a miracle she did not die from blood loss. Mama recovered but never forgot the tortuous birth.

When Carmen was three, the couple decided to build a new home. They had stayed on the family farm. With a lot of hard labor, using stones from the grounds, they constructed a more comfortable home. The old house where they had lived was converted to raise and shelter animals. It was a good business decision as sheep, cows, chickens, and ducks were all raised and then sold to help meet the needs of the family.

Pat was born five years later. Once again Mama's birthing experience progressed badly. She was very late; her body could barely hold such a big baby. And when labor finally began, the midwife suspected it was going to be another tough delivery. Again Grandmother Grazia attended the long, torturous birth. A non-breathing baby came into sight with the cord wrapped around his neck. Pat made Carmen look small; his weight came in at about 13 pounds. With the baby finally out of danger and breathing normally, Grandmother Grazia told Mama in no uncertain terms, "Angela, don't think about having any more children because I can't take another birth like this!"

EMIGRATION

Soon after Angela and Nicola married, they had initiated plans to emigrate. Pat recalls how the trip was delayed. "They applied for passage but did not get an answer until years later when I was six and Carmen was eleven. When the letter giving permission for the family to travel, aunts and uncles and grandparents had already immigrated to the United States."

The letter they received stated the family had four months to make a decision. Nicola was reluctant. He wasn't sure if he wanted to leave the new house and the farm. Mama knew this was her opportunity. The family would move. She packed up their belongings and told the relatives that they would leave.

Pat says, "I did not understand at the time that it would be a long time before I would be able to return." The disquiet did not stop there. "My great aunt told me how the United States fought in wars. She sat me down and explained it this way, 'You will have to go and fight a war for the United States, maybe it will be better if you stay here." Apparently she did not want young Pat to go, she would miss him. The night before the family took leave, all the neighbors and friends came over and lots of food was served throughout the night. Mama was ready for the voyage and ready for a new life.

Arriving in the United States in 1968

At 31 years of age, Angela had big ideas for the future. She frequently told her sons, "You will have a better life in the United States." Letters she received over the years from her family boasted of great schools, business opportunities, and jobs! On the boat conditions were brutal. Crossing high seas Pat witnessed his mother crying, being both sick and sad at losing the only life she had known. Pat stayed close to his big brother Carmen, his best buddy; Carmen, almost a foot taller, was big and strong for his age. He was boisterous and extroverted while Pat exhibited a quieter personality. During that long trip across the ocean they became joined at the hip, telling each other stories in the dark as the wind whistled outside.

Once in America, with the help of Uncle Philip who sponsored the couple, Nicola found employment quickly at the Baldwin School as a bus driver. After a year he moved into the position of grounds keeper at the Mitchell School in Haverford. Mama worked for a furrier, sewing pelts into coats by day and in the evenings she took Pat with her to work at the Mitchell School cleaning classrooms.

While still in Italy Angela had heard about a machine used to make tortellini, and she hoped to find out more and possibly purchase the machine once she had settled in the United States. Pat explains, "She'd talk about her aspirations, but with the reality of raising kids and managing daily life in a new country, it just was not possible to start a new venture."

The couple worked long hours in order to send money back to Italy where they had debt. In 1980 when the school went bankrupt, Nicola was out of a job. In this same time period Mama's cooking was overflowing the family's space.

Carlino's Begins

Pat Carlino's dream bubbled up like a hot tomato sauce on the stove. He visualized a small market offering Mama's pasta, homemade, the old way. As a boy he had interviewed a local deli owner about his business and had written a paper on the topic. It was an A plus project! He felt powerfully optimistic. With organization and help from family he'd make it a reality.

A partnership was born. Having finished his degree at Villanova University, Pat seized the opportunity. In 1983 Mama, Nicola, Pat, and Carmen opened a storefront only a block away from their home in Ardmore. The wooden sign read: "Homemade Pasta."

One year later Carmen ended an affiliation with his uncle and came on board full time to strengthen the team.

The Carlino's original awning- 1986

The original Carlino's sign- 1983

The following are some of the early recipes Mama used.

"The technique is tough. It's all in how you make it."

~ Laura Carlino

Pizza Scima

(Silly Pizza)

❧ Yields: 1 Pizza | Time: 45 minutes ❧

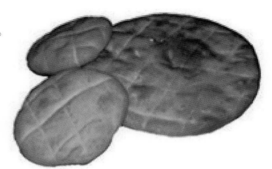

INGREDIENTS:

2 pounds all purpose flour
2 ounces Extra Virgin Olive Oil
2 ounces dry white wine
1 teaspoon baking powder
2 teaspoons salt
water

DIRECTIONS:

1. Pour flour onto a wooden board and make a well in the center.

2. In the center of the well add the olive oil and wine. Start mixing in the flour.

3. Add the baking powder and salt.

4. As the dough is coming together pour a small amount (about 6 teaspoons) of water, enough so that the dough becomes smooth and elastic.

5. Flatten out the dough with a rolling pin to about 1 inch thickness.

6. Place the dough onto an oiled baking sheet, and score it with a serrated knife to create a criss-cross pattern.

7. Bake at 250°F for about 30- 35 minutes, or until golden.

8. Let cool before breaking apart with your hands.

Enjoy this lightly leavened "pizza" with a good sharp cheese such as Auricchio Provolone or Gran Pecorino Carlino.

After about a year, in 1984, Mama launched her talents into the center stall at the farmer's market, in Downingtown, Pennsylvania. Three times a week Mama, Pat, and Laura would pack up what she needed and make the trek. In the midst of a bustling crowd, Mama mixed up a sweet batter, expertly worked it to perfection, and then popped it into the pizzelle iron. Sweeping pizzelle out of the iron she'd lay the crispy, tender morsels on a napkin and hand it to the people waiting. "Wanna taste?" she'd ask.

People flocked to the stand. "Pizzelle" became so popular the announcer at the market would shout to the crowds "Mama Carlino is baking. Get them while they're hot!"

Normally reserved, Mama stretched out of her comfort zone and into a more elastic personality. Pat explains, "Discovering new layers of herself, she thrived in the fast pace." Oozing personality, she kissed babies and worked the crowd like a politician in the throes of a campaign fever. In Mama's case she was campaigning her passion.

The name Mama Carlino stuck. "After that," Pat Carlino says with a wide grin, "you couldn't keep her away from the people."

A typical day in Mama's life began around 3:30 or 4:00 a.m. She'd get up and go downstairs to open the store and start coffee. Chef Luigi or her brother Frank would be waiting for her and they'd share coffee. When the bakers came in she would instruct them. Then she might catch a quick nap before returning to greet her sons as they began their workday.

If she was not cooking, she could be found in her usual spot behind the counter helping customers. If customers came in holding a baby, Mama, all puffed up with maternal nurturing, would offer her loving arms to hold the baby while the parents shopped. Babies loved being comforted in Mama's bosom.

At 3:00 p.m. she decided on a menu for the family's dinner. Going through the store she'd gather her ingredients and then head for home. A grandchild, if available, would help her with dinner preparations. Dinner would be on the table around 6:00 p.m. And all members of the family would be expected to be there on time.

New creations happened at dinnertime. Mama would present her new creation to her family and assorted friends. Likes and dislikes were opinioned. Thumbs up and she'd make it for the store the next day, thumbs down, back to the drawing table. Mama took people's comments seriously as dedicated taste testers. They were an important resource.

Mama Carlino making her famous pizzelle at the Downingtown Farmer's Market- 1984

Pizzelle

Yield: 8 dozen | Time: 1 hour

INGREDIENTS:

1 dozen eggs (large)
5 cups sugar
1 pound butter melted
6 teaspoons baking powder
7 cups flour
3 teaspoons vanilla
Anise seeds (optional)

DIRECTIONS:

1. Melt butter and set aside.

2. Beat eggs and sugar until light and fluffy.

3. Add melted butter and flour alternately.

4. Mix in anise seeds, if using. Batter should be thicker than cake batter.

5. Let batter stand for 10 minutes.

6. Spray griddle with cooking spray for the first pizzelle only.

7. When the machine is ready, drop 1 heaping teaspoon of batter into the center of each griddle.

8. Press the lid down and secure. Cook for about 30 seconds.

9. The pizzelle should be a light, golden color when done.

10. Transfer to a wire cooling rack to cool.

These cookies are delicious eaten as is. For a variety, Mama Carlino loved to sandwich chocolate hazelnut spread between two pizzelle to make the perfect dessert.

Pizzelle

Tuscan Bean and Farro Soup

❧ Serves: 6-8 | Time: 1 ½ hours ❧

INGREDIENTS:

1 cup dry farro
1 pound dry cannellini beans, rinsed
28 ounce can chopped tomatoes
   with juice
¼ cup tomato paste
1 cube vegetable bouillon

½ cup Extra Virgin Olive Oil
2 stalks celery, diced
1 large carrot, diced
1 medium onion, diced
2 tablespoons dried marjoram
Salt and pepper, to taste

DIRECTIONS:

1. Bring a small pot of water to a boil. Reduce to simmer to add to soup if
    necessary later.

2. In a large pot, sauté onions, celery, carrots and beans in olive oil until vegetables
    become soft.

3. Add farro, tomatoes, tomato paste, bouillon and 6 quarts water to the pot and
    stir all ingredients together.

4. Simmer for about 1 hour; adding some boiling water if the liquid begins to
    dissipate.

5. After 1 hour; check the farro and beans to make sure they are tender. If they are
    still hard; continue to cook until they become tender.

6. Add salt to taste.

7. When soup is to your taste; ladle into soup bowls.
    Serve immediately.

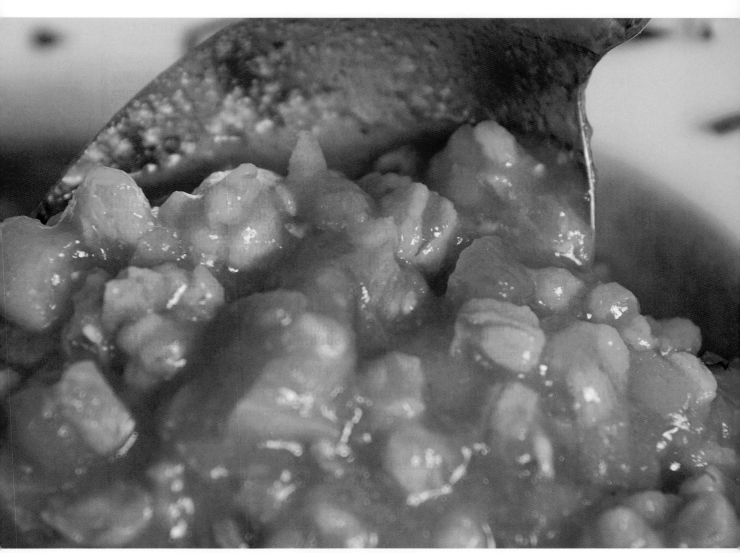

Tuscan Bean and Farro Soup

Pasta per la Pizza Classica

(Classic Pizza Dough)

✎ Yields: 6 pizza dough balls ✎

INGREDIENTS:

¼ cup Extra Virgin Olive Oil

1 ¼ teaspoon instant dry yeast

4 ½ cups Farina 00 (Double Zero Flour)

1 ½ teaspoon salt

1 ¾ cups cold water

DIRECTIONS:

1. To make by hand, combine water, oil and yeast in a large mixing bowl. Add one cup of flour with salt. Gradually continue mixing and adding flour until the dough is too stiff to stir. Knead, adding little flour if necessary, until the dough is elastic (approx. 5 minutes).

2. On the top of the dough, make two incisions that cross, and spread with a very small amount of olive oil.

   This will prevent the surface of the dough from breaking too much while rising.

3. Cover the bowl with a kitchen cloth, and set the bowl aside for approximately 1½ – 2 hours or until the dough doubles in size.

   The time required for rising will depend on the strength of the yeast and the temperature of the room.

4. When the dough is double its original size, punch it down to eliminate the air bubbles.

5. On a lightly floured work surface, cut the dough into equal pieces. You can now use this dough for all of your favorite pizza recipes. Che Bello!

Pasta per la Pizza Classica

Mama's Bolognese Sauce

⤳ Serves: 6-8 | Time: 1 hour ⤳

INGREDIENTS:

4 tablespoons olive oil
1 small onion, finely chopped
1 carrot, finely chopped
1 celery, finely chopped
Handful button mushrooms,
   finely chopped

½ pound lean ground pork
½ pound lean ground beef
½ cup white wine
2 (8 ounce) cans crushed tomatoes
2 tablespoons tomato paste
5-6 fresh basil leaves, roughly chopped

DIRECTIONS:

1. Heat the olive oil in a heavy-bottom skillet over medium heat.

2. Add the onions, carrots and celery; cook until soft.

3. Add the ground meats and cook until no longer pink.

4. Stir in the tomatoes, tomato paste, mushrooms and wine and simmer for about 45 minutes. At 10 minutes before done, add fresh basil, stir, and continue to cook.

5. Toss with any pasta or use to top Polenta su Tavola.

Mama would use this Bolognese Sauce to top short pasta such as penne; for the kids; Angela, Nick, Philip and Nadia.

She especially would make it for Angela when she was little because Angela was such a skinny little girl with "legs like toothpicks" as Mama would lovingly lament!

Mama's Bolognese Sauce

A few years after the store opened when Uncle Frank found himself out of a job, his sister intervened, giving him a place on the Carlino team. Uncle Frank's famous butchering skills were well honed from his days on the farm and his familiarity with rustic cooking allowed him to take on the sauces and soups. But when Frank left for an extended vacation, Mama had to fill the gap so she hired a new chef.

Uncle Frank tells the story of Chef Luigi coming on as an apprentice chef. Uncle Frank is not tall but he has a powerful presence. Humor comes into his eyes when he recalls these events. "I had to go to Australia for one month and when I returned Luigi was in my store wearing my apron! I had been replaced!" Despite the shock he became a guide, showing Luigi the ropes as they shared exhausting twelve-hour days. The room they worked in was small and the ovens produced extreme heat, with room temperatures often approaching 120 degrees.

Laura Carlino remembers the strong personalities and the occasional tempers hotter than the ovens. She said, "Sometimes you break down and cry. But at the end of the day we were all together, a united front." One of the defining characteristics of the emerging business was the ability to increase staff as needed. Certain tasks required different amounts of manpower. "It took ten women and Uncle Frank to make the meatballs." says Laura. She recalls, "As day became night someone would bring out the record player or turn on the radio. As the Italian music began to play, they would sing the old songs." If spirits ran exceptionally high, Frank would get a shine in his eye and dance each woman around the room. As Frank eloquently put it, "Yeah, we had a little fun. It was one way to keep the hard-working women happy!"

Uncle Frank in the kitchen- 1986

CHAPTER FIVE

FAMILY STORIES

ROSANNA

Mama's niece Rosanna DiMedio Shayeghi is Uncle Frank's daughter. She doesn't have to ponder long to come up with her favorite recipe. "PEACHES!" she says with the look of a child receiving her first lollipop. She recalls the years when going to Mama's meant helping her aunt in the kitchen. Rosanna cherished being within the family fold and although Rosanna does not cook professionally she has acquired valuable cooking skills from her much loved aunt.

Her dark hair frames her face as she speaks with clarity. "My aunt was everyone's Mama," she begins. "She had such a big heart; her arms were always open. But she was a serious person at times and had a say if things were not going right.

"I remember my aunt saying to me, 'I have no daughters, so Rosanna is my daughter!' This made me feel special. When she began baking, people immediately wanted to buy her desserts. When large orders came in, we (all the family members) would get the call, `Come help!'"

Rosanna, with light coming up in her dark eyes, happily recounts her love for Mama's Italian wedding peaches' recipe, "This dessert was so ingeniously prepared, no one makes it like her! They are a luscious, gooey, creamy, fruity perfection. In a word, they are magic."

She remembers dipping the formed pastry in glossy red liquor, then rolling it in granular sugar. Draped in their sparkly robes, the peaches mystically turned pink, glistening with sugar. "For the final garnish, we'd go outside and pick leaves from the juniper bush. After washing them, we would place a leaf on each half of the peach. The finished product looked just like a real peach.

"When I grew older and had a car available I chauffeured Mama on shopping trips. Shopping with her required patience, as she liked to compare," she says, smiling.

Rosanna also shared another passion with Mama: travel. "Mama absorbed and explored sights, customs, and FOOD!" She recalls one food-oriented vacation, a cruise. Mama watched closely as the chef carved cantaloupes into elaborate shapes. "You could see the wheels turning and then Mama turned to me and said, `I can do that!' and damn if she didn't the moment she got home."

Rosanna DiMedio Shayeghi

Mama on a visit back to Italy

Mama's Wedding Peaches

INGREDIENTS:

SYRUP

4 cups sugar
4 cups water
2 cups vermouth

½ vanilla bean, scraped
½ cinnamon stick
Orange and yellow food coloring

DIRECTIONS:

1. Place all ingredients in a heavy, medium-sized pot.

2. Boil until the syrup is reduced by half.

3. Cool syrup and add orange and yellow food color to reach desired color.

The Cookies

❧ Yield: 1 dozen | Time: 45 minutes ❧

INGREDIENTS:

COOKIES

4 eggs
1 ¼ cups sugar
¾ cup milk

¾ cup vegetable oil
1 ¼ tablespoons baking powder
Flour, to texture

DIRECTIONS:

1. Preheat oven to 350°F.

2. Whip the eggs and the sugar on high with an electric mixer until the eggs triple in volume and mixture is light and fluffy. Keep whipping until the yolks form ribbons when drizzled from the whisk.

3. Lower speed to medium and add the oil, milk, and vanilla while the yolks are still whipping. Add the baking powder and about 1 cup flour to form loose dough. The cookie dough will be very sticky.

4. Turn the dough out onto a floured surface and slowly knead in more flour until soft dough is formed.

   These cookies are light and soft so it is very important not to overwork the dough.

5. Using a small cookie scoop, drop dough onto a slightly greased cookie sheet spacing them about 2 inches apart.

6. Bake for about 10-12 minutes or until lightly browned around the edges.

7. Remove cookies from the cookie sheet and cool completely on wire cookie rack.

TO ASSEMBLE THE ITALIAN PEACHES:

Crema Pasticcera (1 full recipe), prepared *(refer to page 149)*
Syrup, prepared
Cookies, prepared

3 cups granulated sugar, placed in a shallow bowl
12 Mint (or any other decorative leaves)

DIRECTIONS:

1. Take a cooled cookie in hand and turn it over. Using a teaspoon, scoop out a small hole in the middle of the bottom side of the cookie.

2. Dunk the cookie into the vermouth syrup and hold it submerged until it has taken up as much liquid as it can hold.

3. Remove cookie and let drain on a wire rack for about 20 minutes.

4. Repeat Steps 1-3 for each remaining cookie.

5. Using a teaspoon, fill the center of each cookie with the Crema Pasticcera, and then gently put two cookies together to form a peach shape.

6. Hold the peach in your hands and roll into sugar.

7. Garnish with 2 leaves to complete the peach.

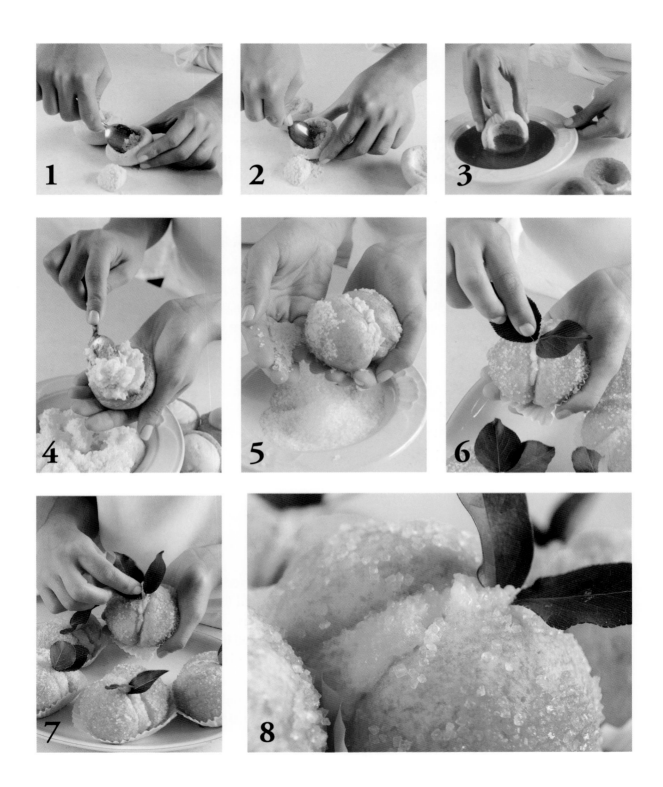

LAURA

Many thousands of loosely connected Italian families emigrated from the Abruzzo region of Italy to the Philadelphia area. Laura DiNardo's family settled in the town of Wayne, about ten miles west of Ardmore. Both families were among those who came from Abruzzo region and their paths soon crossed. When Laura's family needed special desserts they knew the place to acquire the best Italian goodies: Mama's kitchen!

Laura loved tagging along with her mother. At each visit she'd image Aladdin's cave, filled with edible treasures. The baking area was filled with the rich buttery smell of cookies and she wondered . . . would Mama have a candy in her pocket? Or a cookie?

The two families had much in common and as months passed friendships flourished. The DiNardo boys developed tight friendships with Carmen and Pat and they often played bocce together in the long summer evenings at the Italian American Club located next to the store. The families also enjoyed joint celebrations of birthdays and other holidays.

When it came time to open the store, Mama offered Laura a job. Laura fit in handily with the hard-working family. She learned the routines and took pride in her accomplishments within the business. She had started college but working at Carlino's seemed a higher goal, and it won over college. Following the Italian tradition she stayed home while she worked.

One summer 18-year-old Laura sparked a friendship with Carmen. Seven years older than Laura, he was more mature than most of the young men her age, which gave him an advantage. Soon, chemistry flowed between the two like white glaze poured over a Bundt cake. With Mama's keen eye trained on them it was not too long before she asked, "OK, you two, when is the wedding?"

With a pink glow settling on her cheeks, Laura fondly remembers the engagement party Mama and her own mother Santa DiNardo prepared for her. The two mothers orchestrated a beehive of activity, resulting in "mountains and mountains of food!" Laura says with a chuckle, "Nothing is small with us." One hundred women enjoyed a luncheon including hot holiday soup, homemade pasta, roast pork sandwiches with broccoli rabe and hard provolone, and cold salads." After the traditional feast mounds of Mama's handmade cookies and pastries were passed around. As a final offering, the piece de resistance was a huge white tray decorated with white tulle around the edges and holding dozens of "peaches." This queenly dessert took many hands and was a two-to-three day process to make.

Laura was honored with another Italian tradition, the pupa doll.

The pupa doll was one of Mama's more elaborate creations. According to Laura, the doll's colorful costume was designed to reflect an old-style skirt Mama probably saw as a child in Italy. This feminine-looking dessert has a rich history. "In the old world the mother of the family would bake the doll or horse cookie," Laura explains, "with an intention of giving it to a girlfriend or an intended. The most beautiful doll was considered a real coup for a young lady." Laura continues, "And boys received equally impressive horse-shaped creations."

After the wedding, following established traditions Laura moved into the Carlino home. "Many people would not want to live with their mother-in-law," Laura acknowledges, "but Mama had such a warm, welcoming personality that she made me feel comfortable. She taught me so much about life, not only about cooking but also about entertaining and the proper way to do things."

"The pupa doll Mama made me was so special! "- Laura

Pupa or Cavallo Cookie

(Giant Doll or Horse Cookie)

"This is a classic recipe from Abruzzo. Mama used to make them around Easter season. She would give them to her grandchildren as Easter gifts. Traditionally it is made in a doll (pupa) shape for the girls. The little girls carry their dolls around carefully so they don't drop them and break them. She would make them in horse shape (Cavallo) for the boys.

Mama would color the frosting for these cookies, so that her grandchildren could "dress" their dolls however they'd liked."- Chef Jessica

⚬ Yield: 2-4 dolls 12" size | Time: 1 ½ hour total time ⚬

INGREDIENTS:

COOKIES

4 eggs
1 ¼ cups sugar
¾ cup milk
¾ cup vegetable oil
1 ¼ tablespoons baking powder
Flour to texture

FROSTING

3 cups confectioners' sugar
¼ cup water
¼ teaspoon lemon oil
½ teaspoon lemon zest

Pupa Doll

Cavallo

DIRECTIONS:

1. Preheat oven to 350° F.

2. Whip the eggs and the sugar on high with an electric mixer until the eggs triple in volume and mixture is very light and fluffy. Keep whipping until the yolks form ribbons when drizzled from the whisk.

3. Lower speed to medium and add the oil, milk, and vanilla while the yolks are still whipping

4. Add the baking powder and about a cup of flour to form very loose dough. The cookie dough will be very sticky. Turn the dough out onto a floured surface and slowly knead in more flour until soft dough is formed. These cookies are very light and soft so it is very important to not overwork the dough.

5. Place dough on a lightly greased cookie sheet.

6. Using your hands, form dough into a doll or horse shape.

7. Bake for about 12-15 minutes or until lightly browned around the edges.

8. Remove cookies from the cookie sheet and cool completely on wire cookie rack.

HOW TO MAKE LEMON FROSTING FOR PUPA DOLL:

1. Combine confectioners' sugar, water, lemon zest, and lemon oil in a bowl and whisk until smooth. Color frosting if you'd like. Enjoy "dressing" your Pupa with loved ones!

Pat Carlino in Downingtown Farmer's Market at the Carlino's stand

Mama's sons, Pat and Carmen

Pat Carlino

Pat

Pat Carlino, as owner/operator of Carlino's, has a myriad of responsibilities, including quality control, major hires, major purchases, and researching trends. The duties make for a hectic lifestyle. Despite all, he emits a steady flow of calm. His eyes are clearly focused; his manner is deliberate. In the movie Dances with Wolves, there is a warrior named Quiet One. He is a character short on words, but when he speaks, it is with wisdom and sensitivity. When Pat speaks to you, his depth and sincerity are apparent.

His pride and devotion to his family, particularly his children, are also evident. Pat, like his Mama, strongly believes that family is the key to a satisfying and fulfilling life. "In the food business," he notes, "one could be out every night going to dinners and networking events, but my wife and I made the choice to be at home or at our children's activities. This helps keep our lives in balance."

Initially, Pat and his older brother Carmen shared responsibilities at the store. Carmen was larger than life, with a wide chest and thick muscular arms. Carmen was a born leader, widely admired in the old neighborhood. He showed no ill effects of the irregular heartbeat that had been diagnosed in childhood, and few people knew that this condition existed. He lived his life in fast-forward serving as first-string kicker on his school's football team and winning numerous competitions in bocce and bowling tournaments.

In August 1990 Carmen and Pat were playing their weekly bowling game. Carmen had just rolled a strike when suddenly a sharp pain hit him and he slumped into a nearby chair. Pat was concerned, "You need to get this checked out!" he insisted. But it was only a week before their bi-annual hunting trip. Carmen insisted it would pass.

The following weekend the Carlino men headed to the Poconos for the scheduled deer-hunting trip. This retreat was a "la grande passione," a great passion! Carmen would check with the doctor when they got home.

Saturday morning broke clear with a blue sky with just a few streaky gray-white clouds. They spent several hours scanning through the trees, straining to hear, with no sightings. Then Pat spotted a few light hoof prints. Quietly he followed the meandering buck well over a mile, waiting for a clean shot. Feeling the trigger with his index finger he slowly squeezed. Bam! It was a hit. The buck collapsed silently to the ground.

That night around the campfire, the guys toasted Pat's success. Congratulations were mixed with ribbing. "That deer just fell into your lap!" one taunted. Carmen raised his large right hand, looking somber. "No," he said. "Pat is not lucky," he said quietly, "Pat is good."

There was a moment of silence. Such a compliment was rare from his older brother. The camaraderie of that moment is still with Pat.

The two brothers had planned to go in different directions the next morning. When Carmen was dressed and ready to leave, he simply paused for a moment and looked at Pat. Then Carmen quickly left for the mountain. "It was odd," Pat says, thinking back. "We always talked in the morning, strategizing for the day. But on this day he left without saying a word."

This morning had dawned muggy and unseasonably hot. Pat and his father stayed close to the camp since one deer was the limit and he could no longer hunt. Carmen and his uncles headed off to another mountain.

Pat remembers the morning clearly in his mind's eye. Legs heavy with heat, they trudged up the trail. When the trail divided, Pat's father took the path leading down into a valley while Pat hiked across the upper field. "For about an hour we traipsed onward. Nothing moved. Then without warning, I felt a bolt of energy, like a whoosh. It just came up, around, and through me. It was an indescribable sensation. My stomach heaved. I felt like the energy was being sucked out of my body. It was like my very soul was being extracted."

Pat glanced down to the trail below and met his father's gaze. "Let's go," Nicola shouted. He had felt something too. The two men rushed to the cabin, packed quickly, and began the five-hour trip home. Both of them felt ill. Like a dark cloud traveling from a distance, they waited and watched. If they had been listening to the radio they might have heard the following announcement: "Man falls off mountain, Carmen Carlino dead at age 33."

No one had heard the announcement. "Where's my Daddy?" three-year-old Angela asked her Uncle Pat after they had returned to Ardmore. "Why isn't he here?" She threw her arms around Pat's neck so hard he had to tell her to stop.

It would be a few hours yet before the uncles returned, bearing grim news. Carmen had apparently collapsed of a massive heart attack. He was gone. At the news too horrendous to take in, Pat sank into a zone of disbelief, imagining his brother strong as a horse, his best buddy, his business partner lying lifeless in the woods. How could they

Laura and Pat at the register, circa 1983

go on without him? Then Pat remembered the whoosh that had come through him in the woods. Given their extremely close connection, he believes he felt on a physical level his brother's spirit leaving.

The family retreated to their homes. Mama collapsed on the couch, her rosary in hand.

Rallying, the family stood together as they received hundreds of family and friends who came by to pay respects for the next two days. Mama suffered the toughest loss, the death of a son. Her deep steadfast faith helped her rise in the morning but in the following weeks and months an anchor of sadness pulled at her. She worried about her daughter-in-law Laura, now a widow and her two young children Nick, 18 months, and Angela, barely three. Even now tears well as Laura remembers their tragic loss. "The store was our livelihood," she explains. "What else could we do? We had no money. We needed to keep going, so we cried and then went back to work."

For weeks Pat lay sleepless at the back of the house. One night he was startled by the sound of his brother's footsteps on the stairs. "The steps came up to my door and stopped," Pat recalls. "I sat up and cried out, 'Carmen, I know you're here . . . but you have to go. I know you have to leave.' Then the steps went down the stairs. I know that it was Carmen's spirit reassuring me he was OK."

With great resilience Laura and Pat together cared for the family and the store. They had come to know each other well and over time they became a couple, finding comfort in their togetherness in the space of their loss.

"Some people think this is unusual," Nick shrugs. "But to my sister and me it seemed a happy and sensible transition."

Pat and Laura were united in marriage in 1993 in the local Catholic church.

Laura described how she and Pat planned for the future. "Both of us come from large loving families. We felt having another child might solidify the family after our loss. And it did bring the family together." Philip was born in 1995. Then a few years later Nadia arrived, dimpled like her dad. "Nadia is the gel!" Laura says, with affection. "From day one, she has had a heart for people."

Laura and Pat's wedding photo

NADIA

Poppop Nicola and Mama had an adoring relationship with Nadia. Nicola's face glows with a smile when he encounters his youngest granddaughter. In his strongly accented voice, he booms, "Stellinna!" Nadia explains her special name. Swinging her ponytail and smiling with confidence, she says, "Poppop thought Mama would become a star because she was such a good cook, and since I worked right along side her, I became 'little star!' He thought we both had star quality." She adds, "With Mama I would never get in trouble for anything I did, she'd let me stay in her arms. I'd sit on her lap and watch the news until it was time to cook dinner. Then I'd help. I liked it when she'd say, 'One day you will be a great chef if you cook from your heart.'" Nadia shares her grandmother's confidence. "One day I am going to be a main chef."

During the hot and humid Philadelphia summers, Philip and Nadia spent free time outside on the patio and in the pool. Often Mama would relax in the sunshine and watch the kids playing in the pool. Sometimes she would even join them in the water. Nadia would lean back in Mama's arms and watch the puffy white clouds while Mama sang to her, in Italian, of course. But Mama stayed only in the shallow end as she never learned to swim.

Sometimes the family enjoyed a boisterous game of Scope, an Italian card game. Nadia demonstrates how to play the card game by pulling out the small cards one by one. Her eyes flash with fun as she says, "Each symbol is matched with a like symbol, and at the end of the game we count up the points." Then she lowers her voice, "Mama always let me win," she confides.

Coming home from school Nadia has her priorities in order: she promptly calls her Mom and says, "I'm ready to come to the store!" As soon as she enters the store, she zones in on her two favorite grandmas and dispenses hugs with enthusiasm. Then she begins her "rounds." Starting in the salad department she grabs a flat plate and tongs, then she begins making selections. "The mix," as she calls it, is a combo of Hearty Bean Salad (mix of five beans with extra virgin olive oil dressing), Tuna Salad, Cheese Tortellini with broccoli and feta cheese, and one cherry sized (cilegine) mozzarella ball-- and don't forget the roll. "Mama used to make the same mix," she says. Why not? It's a great way to check the inventory!

After checking up on the other departments, Nadia skips down the aisles making her way to the bakery case. Peering in to the creative, colorful adventures in cake and icing, she faces a tough choice. Which one will it be? A baby chocolate cupcake apparently has her name on it.

PHILIP

Many of the Carlino family members are like peas in a pod. But one pea jumped ship. Nadia's brother Philip has interests that tend in a different direction. Although he adores homemade pasta and gelato, he is the rogue Carlino. As a boy he loved animals and he has thought about becoming a veterinarian. Also, like his Dad he is captivated by the sport of baseball. He says, in a calm thoughtful voice, "My perfect career might involve combining interests in writing and baseball."

Philip, Mama, Nadia and Nicola

Philip and Mama

Nadia, Nick and Philip

Nadia and Philip

Arancini di Riso

(Stuffed Rice Balls)

≈ Serves: 6 | Time: 40 minutes ≈

INGREDIENTS:

BREADING

1 cup coarse bread crumbs

FILLING

2 cups cooked risotto rice, cooled
½ cup bread crumbs
½ cup finely grated Parmigiano
   Reggiano Cheese
¼ cup finely chopped fresh basil leaves
¼ finely chopped fresh Italian parsley

NOTES:

Depending on the type of Gorgonzola you use, you may have a salty or less finished product. We recommend using Gorgonzola "Dolce", a creamy, lower-sodium cheese imported from either Lombary or Piedmonte, Italy.

2 eggs, at room temperature, beaten
4 ounces Gorgonzola, at room
   temperature, cut into 16 (½ inch)
   cubes
1 cup frozen green peas, thawed
Canola oil for frying

DIRECTIONS:

1. Breading: Add the bread crumbs to a medium bowl. Set aside.

FILLING

1. In a medium bowl, combine the risotto, bread crumbs, Parmigiano Reggiano cheese, basil, parsley, peas, and eggs.

2. With damp hands, using about 2 tablespoons of the risotto mixture, form the mixture into 1 ¾-inch diameter balls.

3. Make a hole in the center of each ball and insert a cube of Gorgonzola. Cover up the hole to completely enclose the cheese. Roll one ball at a time in the breading to coat.

4. In a large heavy-bottomed saucepan, pour in enough oil to fill the pan about ⅓ of the way. Heat over medium heat until a deep-frying thermometer inserted in the oil reaches 350° F. (If you don't have a thermometer, a cube of bread will brown in about 2 minutes.) In batches, fry the rice balls, turning occasionally, until golden, about 4 to 5 minutes. Drain on paper towels and serve.

Italian Love Cake

ITALIAN LOVE CAKE

∾ Serves: 10-12 | Time: 20 minutes ∾

This is a recipe that Rosanna adapted from one of Mama's more elaborate creations.

INGREDIENTS:

1 box of marble cake mix
2 pounds of ricotta cheese
4 eggs
¾ cup of sugar
1 teaspoon vanilla

1 cup of milk
1 (4 ounce) box of instant chocolate pudding mix
8 ounces of store-bought whipped topping

DIRECTIONS:

1. Preheat oven to 350°F.

2. Begin preparing marble cake mix. Follow the box instructions using 2 eggs instead of the recommended 3.

3. Pour batter into a 13" x 9" greased and floured pan.

4. Mix together ricotta cheese, eggs, sugar and vanilla.

5. Pour mixture over cake batter.

6. Bake for at least 1 hour or until the cake no longer jiggles.

7. Cool for 1 ½ hours then refrigerate overnight. This allows flavors to blend and cake to settle.

FOR THE TOPPING: *(Add the topping about one hour before serving)*

1. Hand mix milk with entire contents of the instant chocolate pudding mix.

2. Fold in 8 ounces of cool whip topping.

3. Refrigerate again until ready to serve.

Mama at age 5 dressed as an angel for a church function

Chapter Six

Mama's Faith

Mama had grown up in pre-World War II Italy and Catholicism was engrained in her soul. She held it like a baby, close to her heart. Her faith offered clarity and confidence, a path through the challenges in Italy as well as America. Granddaughter Nadia, remembers, "Mama loved to pray several times a day." And she always had a symbol of her faith on her person, Big Blue, a rosary notable for its beautiful pearly color.

Mama's family of origin, the DiMedios, was dedicated to St. Gabriel, the patron saint of communication who is commonly known as God's messenger. Perhaps he inspired Mama's warm communication skills. When Angela and Nicola moved to the Philadelphia area, they began attending church at Our Mother of Good Council in Bryn Mawr, Pennsylvania. This beautiful old church, with its lofty ceiling and marble altars infused them with a sense of belonging. It served as a bridge, connecting them with their Italian root. Through the years they would develop a deep and lasting friendship with head pastor James Martinez, known as Father Jim.

In the traditional Italian way Mama had no reservations about mixing business and religion. On Ash Wednesday Father Jim would appear at Carlino's in full regalia. He would press his thumb into the ashes and walk around to each employee, Catholic or not, and bless him with a cross on the forehead while Mama beamed. Mama's faith also extended into other parts of daily life.

Laura Carlino describes the altar in her bedroom, "There was a table in the corner, which held a holy candle and prayer cards, a private place for prayer." The cards, which were dedicated to Saint Padre Pio, were particularly important in Mama's life. Laura's eyes sparkle as she recounts how Mama would carefully wrap the small pieces of cardboard in Saran Wrap. She wanted to be certain that they were airtight and safe. "Then," Laura remembers fondly, "she would deftly tuck a card into her ample bra along with other necessities. If she met someone she deemed needy, Mama would retrieve the card from its safe haven and press it lovingly into that person's hands."

Mama and Laura at the celebration dinner for Pat and Laura's marriage- 1993

Pat continues to carry one of the aged prayer cards encased in a protective plastic folder. It is crumpled around the edges, but the image of a full-faced young man illuminated with a golden halo remains clear and mesmerizing. Pat explains, "My grandmother gave this card to my mother when I was born and Mama gave it to me on my first communion."

Saint Pio was a particularly revered saint in Mama's part of Italy. He was born in 1887 in Pietrelcina, a mere 15 miles from Mama's home. At some point in his life, he received the stigmata, copies of the wounds that Jesus bore. Mama believed that the saint had special qualities to help, especially in times of stress. He was purported to have the gift of reading souls, along with the ability to be in two places at once. On June 16, 2002, he was canonized by Pope John Paul ll.

Mama quoted the saint's words frequently to her family. "Pray, hope, and don't worry." She also enjoyed giving gifts with the saint's likeness. Chef Luigi proudly displays a gold pendant, which he wears frequently. He tells the story of Mama surprising him on Christmas with a large framed rendering of the saint's likeness, which now hangs in his living room.

Of course, for important life events, Mama was there with her blessings. When Angela acquired her first car, her sun visor was decorated with medallions of saints. A rosary twinkling with light swung from the mirror. Prayer cards were stashed in the glove compartment. Angela continues the tale, "Six months after I got the car, I had an accident. In those few seconds before impact it felt like slow motion. I was scared to death but in the back of my mind I knew Mama's accoutrements were with me and I would survive." The car took a double hit on the front and the side, but miraculously Angela walked away without a bruise.

St. Raphaela Retreat House

In preparation for this book, Nick pulled out boxes of photographs and memorabilia stowed in Mama's bedroom. He came across a flyer for an event at St. Raphaela Retreat House, dated 1987. It was a treasure, for this retreat house became central to Mama's life. The stately stone mansion located in Haverford is from another era. It sits on a property of nine acres filled with brilliant mature trees and gardens trimmed to perfection. The nuns who run this religious community have a mission to celebrate God in unconditional love by promoting wholeness, peace, and reconciliation.

Mama was drawn to it, like a pull from moon to a planet. Saint Raphaela offers retreats to parish groups and college students and welcomes over 5,000 guests and visitors per year. For Mama it offered a place of integrity, quiet, and solace. Over the years Mama developed lasting bonds with the nuns, in particular Sister Philomena, who worked within the stately walls.

At 95 years old and four foot nine she is lean and spirited. Her persona is one of dedication. Philomena knows the place inside and out and adores giving tours. Slowly walking the carpeted hall she shares her memories of Mama. "I've known Mama Carlino for over twenty years. She'd come every day rain or shine, right through this door," she says pointing to a side entrance.

Sister Margaret Scott joins Philomena and remembers Mama as well. Proceeding down an elegant hall she points out a mix of exquisite architecture and functionality. In one room a group of Buddhists sits cross-legged on the floor transfixed in a meditation pose.

The property is juxtaposed to a residential area. A short time after Mama discovered St. Raphaela, the family decided it was time for a new residence. Ironically a handsome four-bedroom home directly behind the mansion came up for sale. This comfortable home suited the Carlinos perfectly and they happily purchased the property. Thus began a daily ritual for Mama. Outside, the rolling grounds hold small enclaves with statues and benches for private reflection. One can visualize Mama on a bench, head bowed, holding her big blue rosary in her hand, a serene contrast to her busy life.

Sister Philomena stands by a row of tall sun-filled windows. She pats the seat of a chair and says softly, "This was her spot to talk with the Lord." She pauses, perhaps reminiscing, and then Sister Philomena walks reverently down the bright hallway. She stops at a carved door and pulls it open to reveal a small chapel. The round room is lightly furnished with a simple alter, a few chairs, and several statues. Touching a delicately carved wooden statue she continues, "Mrs. Carlino often brought purple flowers to place here in front of the Blessed Mother."

Glass windows offer a panoramic view of the grounds from inside the circular room. A grotto tucked among the mature oaks can be seen in the distance. Here Mother Mary stands in tranquil solitude. Sister Philomena whispers, "Her hands are cracked due to time and elements." But a repair is in the works, funded by a donation in both of Nick's grandmothers' names.

Sister Margaret only knew Mama for a short time, but they shared respect and affection for each other. She exudes wisdom as she says, "Mrs. Carlino began a tradition of contributing fresh meals for the nuns on Sundays. What a gracious woman." Nick carries on the tradition, personally delivering hot meals each Sunday.

Nick also seems to find a sense of peace here within the walls of this sacred place. As he sits listening to the stories told by the nuns, he remembers one of his own. "Mama wanted a private path leading from the family's backyard to the retreat house. It made perfect sense. We cleared a path and planted colorful flowerbeds on either side so Mama could stroll though the garden and into her place of prayer."

Each year an event called the Italian Day of Prayer was scheduled. The highlight was a Mass said in Italian. Mama planned and implemented the luncheon for the event and enjoyed seeing many family and friends in attendance. Sister Margaret clasps her hands together and confides, "Mrs. Carlino was an apostle in her way, through the store and here at the retreat house."

In the depth of winter Mama often made vegetable soup for the nuns who especially loved this warming nurturing food.

Minestrone alle Fave

(Vegetable Soup with Fava Beans)

Serves: 4-6 | Time: 45 minutes

INGREDIENTS:

½ cup Extra Virgin Olive Oil
1 small onion, peeled and diced
1 fennel bulb, ends trimmed,
   thinly sliced
2 garlic cloves, peeled and minced
3 medium tomatoes, peeled, seeded,
   and coarsely chopped
2 carrots, peeled, ends trimmed,
   cut into ¼-inch dice
2 celery stalks, diced

2 small, firm zucchini, ends trimmed,
   cut into ¼-inch dice
8-10 fresh basil leaves
5 cups water
½ head escarole, washed, bruised leaves
   removed, and shredded
1 cup shelled fava beans, skins of beans
   removed
½ cup tubetti pasta
Salt and freshly ground black pepper
   to taste

DIRECTIONS:

1. Heat the olive oil in a large soup pot.

2. Add the onion and cook over moderate heat until it starts to become translucent.

3. Add the fennel and sauté until it is just tender but not completely soft.

4. Add the garlic and cook for about 5-7 minutes or until just browned.

5. Add the chopped tomatoes and cook for about 5 minutes or until tomatoes begin to break down and give off their juices.

6. Add the carrots and celery, and gently sauté for 5 minutes.

7. Add the zucchini and basil, and sauté for an additional 5 minutes.

8. Add the water and bring to a boil.

9. Add the escarole and fava beans. Turn down heat and simmer for approximately 20 minutes or until all vegetables are tender. Season to taste with salt and pepper.

10. Add the tubetti pasta approximately 10 minutes before the end of the cooking time, stirring frequently.

Mama would make this recipe heartier by sautéing 4-5 oxtails with 2-3 shallots and 3 garlic cloves with ¼ cup vegetable oil; then continue from Step 1.

At the end of the cooking time, just before adding the pasta; remove the oxtails from soup with a slotted spoon, shred into pieces, discard fat, and add back to the soup.

CHAPTER SEVEN

THE WAY YOU MADE ME FEEL

"There are many, many people who called Mama their best friend."

~ Pat Carlino

"I've learned that people will forget what you said, and people will forget what you did, but people will never forget how you made them feel."

~ Maya Angelou, poet/writer

"This quote is how I think of Mama Carlino! She made me feel like I was back with my grandmother," says Michael Colleran, a dear friend for more than 30 years. Michael, a slim runner type and an elegant man, met the Carlinos soon after they opened their storefront in Ardmore. He was working as a network TV executive in Philadelphia and usually stopped to pick up dinner for his family several times per week. Currently he is the founder of a new company called InterviewWise. He tells his story of friendship with Angela and Nicola Carlino.

"Mama did not say much, but her gestures equaled love. In my family we are all foodies. I'm from Gessup, Pennsylvania, a tiny coal-mining town near Scranton. We lived in the Italian section of town and my grandmother made the traditional foods. I'm Irish by birth, Italian by love.

"I was thrilled to discover Carlino's in Ardmore," he says as his eyes express anticipation of good eating. "That first night, as I devoured pasta smothered in genuine Italian marinara sauce accompanied by asparagus drizzled with fresh pressed Carlino's olive oil, I said, 'I'm home . . . this is my grandmother's food.'" Soon these new acquaintances evolved into enduring friendships with Angela and Nicola.

Michael's voice crackles with nostalgia and tears brim in eyes when he says, "I will never forget the time I was visiting with Nicola and he suddenly held up his hand and said, 'Wait.' He left for a minute then he came out from behind the counter with his

Mama, niece Anna Vuono, and Laura hand-rolling the baby meatballs used in the famous Holiday Soup

hands outstretched; his eyes held a look of elation. He had a surprise for me. As he came closer I recognized a set of large old-fashioned metal keys in his cupped palms."

"He held them out to me, as if making an offering, and in a mild bellow said, 'Keys! Keys to the family farm! You go. You see. You touch!' He was offering me the keys to his farm in Italy." Michael stops and pauses, "I never did visit the family farm, but I was deeply touched by the offer."

Angela used a similar gesture to convey her caring. Michael continues, "When I'd come into the store she'd say, 'God bless. How the children?' I would finish my shopping and be passing the bakery, and she would approach me with her hands out holding a biscotti or two on a square of waxed paper. 'For you, for family, God bless.'"

Another couple that was to become instrumental in the lives of the Carlino family was Kathy and John DiMichele. Kathy was hired to work in the store office shortly after they moved from Canada to Ardmore. In mere nanoseconds, she felt drawn to the Carlino clan. Kathy says, "One can only hope to meet such people. Mama took us under her wing."

She and her husband John also established a close connection with Pat and Laura. Pat describes how John filled a gap in his life. "After my brother Carmen passed away, I felt very protected, guarded with the Italian community. It was as if I lived in a glass jar with people always looking in. Everything was so public."

When Carmen was alive, in his bold loving way he had a way of drawing Pat out. For some time Pat had retreated, often seeming far away. Swinging into Ardmore, high-spirited John pumped energy back into Pat. John is average height but not average in any other way. Like a rollicking clown he talks in a lighthearted tone, telling stories about Mama. "I used to love to make her laugh. She impressed me first as the matriarch of the family. In the store nothing was done without her stamp of approval."

John describes the link between the two families. "I think our families hit it off because we have an Italian bond; my parents came from the town of St. Gabrielle in Abruzzo, not far from Casoli. When we first met Mama, she welcomed us like we were long lost friends, and that's how it should be!" When Laura and Kathy both became pregnant in the same year, they decided each would become godparents to the other's child. After the christening John became known as Compare, a sign of respect.

About two months after John and Kathy's son was born, it was discovered he had autism and hemophilia, a blood disorder. The Carlino family took matters into their own hands and established a yearly golf outing to raise funds in support of needy children and families dealing with this blood disorder. Mama spearheaded the luncheon and was there to personally serve all the golfers. Pat remembers her "serving up a storm and then coming back to help with the dinner at night." The money collected during the day was given to Mama for safekeeping until it could be counted and passed on to the foundation. He said, "No one came near Mama's pocketbook!"

For a number of years the two families attended a special festival. One summer evening they both set off to Saint Gabriele Festival in Broomall, Pennsylvania, which raises money for a church in St. Gabriele, Italy. The music was sparkling. As usual, Kathy and John were out on the dance floor throwing their hair back and limbs around with abandon. Somehow Kathy convinced Pat to join them, and the plug holding in the sadness and restraint loosened. He danced full force as free and wild as a galloping horse. Pat says, "I felt free again, to just do my own thing and not care so much what other people thought."

The next time Mama saw Kathy, she said, "Thank you for bringing my Pat back. It healed my heart to see him dance, to see him live again."

The casinos in Atlantic City, New Jersey, were a popular destination for many families in the area. Pat had introduced his parents to the razzle-dazzle of the slot machines. After Mama got a taste of the slots, she wanted to go back. She was hooked; she also happened to be quite lucky.

One evening the Carlinos and DiMicheles drove into the city together. The two families entered a casino glimmering with action, spilling with lights, smoke, and people in the pursuit of the happy sensation of winning. John and Pat observed Mama loading coins into the slot, pulling the lever down with confidence, watching the spinning cherries, oranges, and bells. Bingo! She was hitting almost every time. Good fortune created a magnetic pull. She yelled heartily each time the coins rattled into the bin!

John, visualizing the scene in his mind's eye, describes Nicola who, hearing the shrieks from round the bend, came to investigate. "Witnessing Mama happily scooping up the clattering coins from the maw of the hungry machines, Nicola slowly wiped his brow before sheepishly mumbling as to how perhaps Mama should share her winnings allowing him to continue to play. She said, 'Winnings?' and cheerily sent him on his way."

Learning the ropes of the game Mama discovered the point system. If she acquired enough points, she could then turn them in for prizes. The prizes included cookware,

Left to right, front: cousin Angelina Carlino, young Angela, Laura, Mama, Carmen
Left to right, back: another cousin, Laura's brother, Nick and Pat

Mama and her father.

Left to right: Laura, John DiMichele, Mama, Pat and Kathy DiMichele

crystal, and cutlery. She couldn't believe it; she traded her points for a beautiful set of cookware. Then she instructed John to stash the cookware in the trunk while the rest of the group was still inside the casino.

When Mama visited John and Kathy for dinner the next week she had a present for them: a set of spanking new pots and pans! Nicola had no idea how she got all the cookware.

In a subdued, wistful tone John concludes, "We still play the slots occasionally but now we play in Mama's memory."

CHAPTER EIGHT

CHEF LUIGI: IT'S MAMA'S WAY.

Executive Chef Louis Pietrantonio's high-amp energy is barely containable; his eyes scan the shelves for anything askew. What's full? What's empty? Who needs help? "You are too much of a stallion," Mama used to say when the young chef came on board. She trained him with a falcon eye. She expected excellence.

"Coming out of culinary school I had no idea!" Luigi says with wide eyes. "I had to start over from square one." He hunches down as if trying to slow himself down. He takes a full breath, stretches to his full height of six foot two inches, and begins with a voice which rolls up and down depending on the event. "In the early days I was the receiver, the coordinator, the go-get guy. If something didn't go right, 'I'd hear 'Luigi did it!' but it was OK."

He says, hands on hips, his face shifting gears, "I developed a passion to learn the old way. Mama gave looks, not many words. She was a powerful force. After all she came from the fields; she'd grab my arm and I'd feel the strength."

He recalls the days in Ardmore when Mama lived on the top floor of the store. "Mama always called me 'Luigi.' I'd be waiting downstairs for her to open up early, around 4:00 a.m. She'd come down, put the coffee on. Then she'd put biscotti in her cup and wait till it was soft and then pop it in her mouth. Over coffee we often discussed food.

"Most of her methods of cooking came from the Abruzzo region, where the food was prepared using what was available. It was extremely important for me to learn her way! 'You gotta listen Luigi,' she'd say.

"She taught me to enjoy and appreciate what I was doing. I developed the passion to learn the old ways from the homeland." Luigi has been with Carlino's 20 plus years. He says, "Mama saw me through some hard times." His voice becomes almost a whisper, "I had some personal difficulty after my father died. She had patience with me; she helped me find a place that feels like my own!"

Mama with Chef Luigi on his wedding day

The Inner Sanctum – The New Carlino's Market in West Chester, Pennsylvania

Luigi takes off like a missile, down a set of stairs, down the hatch to the mammoth-sized kitchen and prep areas, where he manages a staff of bakers and cooks. The long underbelly of the Carlino's new West Chester store is where produce and foodstuffs come in and the recipes come alive.

A succulent roast, beautifully browned, sits "resting" on a metal countertop. Luigi approaches it, leans in, and artistically places the finishing garnish. A cacophony of sounds surrounds him: the chopping of veggies for soup, the pounding of meats, and pans clanking in soapy water. An occasional voice rises as chefs coordinate and assist one another. A muscular chef holds a huge hand-held mixer beating a mixture of ingredients in a large bucket, then pours the contents into a gigantic vat of simmering sauce. Though it is intensely busy there is fluidity to all the movements.

Luigi moves powerfully past the workstations and comes to a stop in a quieter section of the kitchen. His burly frame contrasts to tears forming in his eyes, "It's hard going on without Mama." He straightens his shoulders and says, "When I started 20 years ago we only had three soups, six types of pasta, and two sauces." Striding down the aisle he says, "Now we have approximately 70 people working here in this kitchen."

Uncle Frank points out a huge 60-gallon vat of tomatoes and sauce and explains how the machine is set to keep the sauce at a perfect simmer. At a double gas burner stove Uncle Frank has two kettle-drum sized pots filled to the brim with meatballs and sauce. Heat pours out like an exhaust from a racecar. Looking a bit moist Uncle Frank wears the signature Carlino black chef's cap and carries a large green bottle of "Fiuggi," (a natural Italian water). Holding the bottle he says, "good for hydration!"

Stopping at a station Chef Luigi introduces Gildo DiNardo, Laura's brother and the master mixer of the meatballs. Luigi confides, "Only four people know the ingredients and technique for Mama's secret meatball recipe." Gildo is gracious and owns one of the happiest smiles on earth; he literally glows as he packs a three-foot-high machine with meat mixture. Burrrring, the machine comes to life turning out perfectly sized three-inch balls. Twin meatballs pop out of the bottom and race down a little ramp where they are coaxed by Gildo's hand to line up at the side where they receive a light mist of Carlino's olive oil. Luigi says, "Each meatball receives the touch."

Chef Angela's Melanzana alla Parmigiana

(Eggplant Parmigiana)

 Serves: 6 | Time: 1 hour

INGREDIENTS:

3 medium eggplants
1 tablespoon sea salt
3 large eggs
1 teaspoon salt
All purpose flour for dredging
2 cups fine, dry breadcrumbs
½ cup Extra Virgin Olive Oil or
  as needed

½ cup vegetable oil
5 cups Mama's Basic Tomato Sauce,
  (recipe on page 81)
2 cups grated Parmigiano Reggiano
  cheese
12 basil leaves
1 pound Fresh Mozzarella, cut into slices
  ⅓ inch thick

DIRECTIONS:

1. Trim the stems and ends from the eggplants (cut off the peel in 1 inch strips leaving about half the peel intact.) Cut the eggplant lengthwise into ½ inch thick slices and place them in a colander. Sprinkle with the sea salt and let drain for 1 hour. Rinse the eggplant under cool running water, drain thoroughly and pat dry.

2. Whisk the eggs and 1 teaspoon salt together in a 13 x 9 inch baking pan. Spread the flour and breadcrumbs in an even layer in two separate wide, shallow bowls or over sheets of wax paper. Dredge the eggplant slices in flour, shaking off the excess. Dip the floured eggplant into the egg mixture, turning well to coat both sides evenly. Let excess egg drip back into the pan, then lay the eggplant in the pan of breadcrumbs. Turn to coat both sides well with breadcrumbs, pressing with your hands until the breadcrumbs adhere well to the eggplant.

3. Pour ½ cup each of the olive oil and vegetable oils into a medium skillet. Heat over medium-high heat until a corner of the eggplant slices gives off a lively sizzle when dipped into the oil. Add as many of the eggplant slices as fits without touching, and cook, turning once, until well browned on both sides, about 6 minutes. Remove the eggplant to a baking pan lined with paper towels and repeat with the remaining eggplant slices.

Chef Angela's Melanzana alla Parmigiana

4. Adjust the heat as the eggplant cooks to prevent the bits of coating that fall off the eggplant slices from burning. Add the oil to the pan as necessary during cooking to keep level consistent.

5. Preheat the oven to 375° F. Ladle enough sauce into a 9x13 inch baking dish to cover the bottom. Sprinkle with an even layer of grated cheese and top with a layer of fried eggplant, pressing it down gently.

6. Tear a few leaves of basil over the eggplant and ladle about ¾ cup of the sauce to coat the top evenly. Sprinkle an even layer of grated cheese over the sauce and top with a layer of Mozzarella, using about one-third of the cheese.

7. Repeat the layering as described above two more times, ending with a top layer of sliced cheese that leaves a border of about 1 inch around the edges of the baking dish. Drizzle sauce around the border of the baking dish and sprinkle the top layer with the remaining grated cheese. Finish with a few decorative streaks or rounds of tomato sauce. Cover the baking dish loosely with aluminum foil and poke several holes in the foil with the tip of a knife. Bake 30 minutes.

8. Uncover, and continue baking until the top layer of cheese is golden in spots about 15 minutes. Let rest 10 to 20 minutes, then cut into squares and serve.

Tip: When frying use a spider skimmer to remove bits of breading in between batches to further prevent them from burning.

Uncle Frank interjects with a wink and a smile, "I hate the word "rage!" He adds, "In Italy our family never made meatballs, instead we made polpette, a mixture of ground pork, bread, cheeses, and parsley. It was formed into a small log shape and fried in olive oil. Delizioso!"

Next door Bruno DiNardo, Laura's other brother, has been with Carlino's for 21 years. He carefully pulls rosemary leaves off a stalk. Explaining, he says, "Rosemary is the seasoning for garlic rosemary cheese sticks. We make a ton of them; people special order them for parties." Wafting through the kitchen the smell of baking bread, garlic, basil, rosemary, and tomato sauce create a merry-go-round of aromas.

Chris, a new young baker, has his arms loaded with a massive bucket of a chocolaty mix, which he pours expertly into a large rectangle pan. It's the beginning of a huge sheet cake. Next he begins preparation for peach bundt cakes, adding freshly squeezed lemon juice to cut up peaches. Luigi steps in and reminds him, "Just a little lemon juice, too much and it will change the flavor." Chris nods his head. He is still learning.

Back upstairs on the retail floor is general manager, Nick DiNardo, the youngest of the DiNardo brothers. A key member of the team, he could not be better suited for the job. Running his fingers through his dark abundant hair, he says with understated pride, "At age ten Carmen was like a big brother to me. He showed me the ropes, starting with simple tasks like sweeping floors and stocking shelves. I used to take the bus from Wayne to get to the Ardmore store. Over the years I gained experience in every job in the store."

A customer eyes him and approaches with a question. "What kind of pasta goes well with this pesto sauce?" Nick has the answer. He steers the customer over to the refrigerated fresh pastas. His amiable approach is clearly appreciated and his sense of humor is apparent when he lists the nicknames for family members. He says, "Mama was the backbone; Carmen, the worker bee; Pat, the thinker- finance man; and Laura, the big cheese!" Nick is positive about the future of the stores as he has watched the Carlino enterprise grow and develop a strong customer base. He says with optimism, "People respond to the education and care the staff offers."

Chef Tom staffs the take-out area where about 45 dishes are exquisitely presented: roast duck to vegetable risotto, whipped sweet potatoes, pork with wild mushrooms stuffed with spinach, filet of beef stuffed with cranberries, gorgonzola cheese with a demi-glaze. No winging it for Chef Tom; he knows each dish as well as a sommelier knows wine.

Laura tending to the tortellini machine

Phyllis comes out of the office crammed with computers. As general manager, she organizes a myriad of details. Mama and Phyllis's parents lived near each other in Ardmore and were very close. She recalls Mama being a supportive friend. "When my mother passed away, I told Mama that what I missed most was her cooking. Mama responded by telling me, 'You come over to my house anytime, I will cook for you.' I never forgot that. It was so genuine."

Mama's Basic Tomato Sauce

∾ Yield: 4 cups | Time: 50 minutes ∾

INGREDIENTS:

¼ cup extra virgin olive oil
1 medium onion, diced
4 cloves garlic, thinly sliced
6-8 fresh basil leaves, roughly chopped

2 (28 ounce) cans peeled whole
  tomatoes, crushed by hand and
  juices reserved
Salt, to taste

DIRECTIONS:

1. In a medium saucepan, heat olive oil over medium heat. Add onion and garlic and cook until onion is translucent, being careful not to burn the garlic, about 8-10 minutes. Add the crushed tomatoes and their juice and bring to a boil, stirring often. Lower the heat and simmer for 30 minutes. Add the chopped basil and cook for 5 more minutes. Season with salt.

   Once cooled, this sauce will keep in the refrigerator for 1 week or in the freezer for up to 6 months.

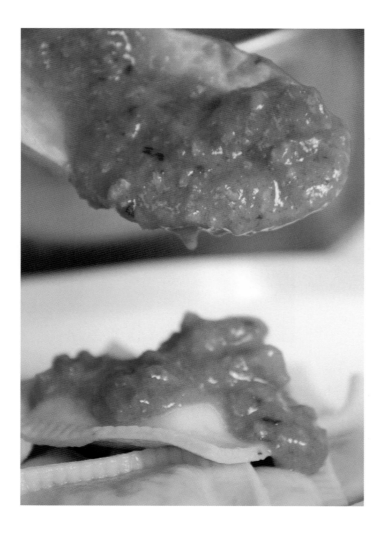

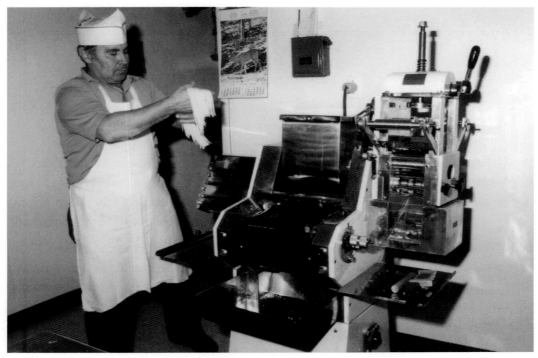

Nicola making the homemade spaghetti- 1983

Mama's father, Alfonso, packaging tortellini- 1983

POLPETTE CLASSICHE

(Classic Meatballs)

Mama Carlino always tried to make her family the most nutritious meals possible. She baked her meatballs using minimum fat, but still was able to achieve a golden brown exterior and fluffy interior, making them the most nutritious and delicious meatballs around!

❧ Yield: 12 meatballs | Time: 25 minutes ❧

INGREDIENTS:

⅓ pound ground pork
⅓ pound ground beef
⅓ pound ground veal
1 ½ cup fine dry bread crumbs
⅔ cup Locatelli Cheese (or Pecorino Romano), freshly grated
¼ cup Italian parsley, chopped

2 garlic cloves, peeled and finely chopped
1 large egg
1 teaspoon salt
¼ teaspoon freshly ground black pepper
¼ cup olive oil
¼ cup vegetable oil

DIRECTIONS:

1. Preheat oven to 375°F (if making baked meatballs).

2. Crumble the beef, pork, and veal into a mixing bowl.

3. Sprinkle the breadcrumbs, grated cheese, parsley and garlic over the meat. Beat the eggs with the salt and pepper in a small bowl until blended. Pour over the meat mixture.

4. Mix the ingredients with clean hands just until evenly blended. Do not over mix.

5. Shape the meat mixture into 1 ½ inch balls, or ¼ inch balls for holiday soup *(recipe on page 109)*.

6. Baked Meatballs: Place meatballs on a greased baking sheet about 1 inch apart. Bake for 30 minutes. Turn meatballs over after 15 minutes.

7. Fried Meatballs: Heat olive oil and the vegetable oil in a large, heavy skillet over medium-high heat. Slip as many meatballs into the skillet as will fit without crowding. Fry, turning as necessary, until golden brown on all sides, approximately 5 minutes. Remove the meatballs and drain on paper towels. Repeat if necessary with the remaining meatballs.

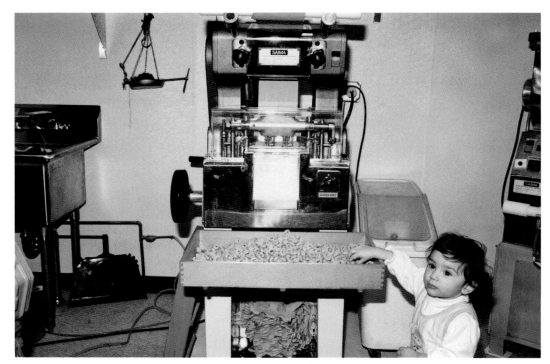

Angela at age 2 eating the freshly made tortellini

Mama whipping up a batch of béchamel sauce

Mama under the Big Lights - Cooking Show

On a quick lunch break Chef Luigi chows down on strawberries and cottage cheese (can you believe it?) while telling the story of Mama under the lights. "Mama really wanted her own TV show. We were thrilled to accept an invitation to appear on Fretz's Kitchen Show, a cooking show filmed in Philadelphia. While I was driving in for the filming we took turns being nervous. Once the cameras were rolling Mama took command of the cooking while I explained her methods. It was a success. We had customers telling us they watched it many times over the years."

Pat also acknowledges Mama's long-held dream. "She wanted a larger audience, but she was self-conscious about the way she spoke. She hoped granddaughter Angela would take on the challenge and she has as chef of our cooking school."

Mama also participated in a show filmed right in her own kitchen. In 2005 Pat worked with a friend who was slated to host a new pilot for cable television. Mama was asked to be a guest on the new show called Famous Chefs' Homes. Each show would feature a chef in her own home, preparing a favorite dish. Pat exuberantly explains, "Mama made eggplant parmigiano, planning every detail including flowers." Laura Carlino acted as narrator, explaining each segment of preparation. As Mama completed her preparation, the camera zoomed in on the presentation. It was a long arduous day of prep and cooking. Pat describes the final shot, "The whole family walked out to the patio and sat down at the table. We popped open a homemade bottle of wine and began the meal. After the crew left, Mama groaned and said 'Oh my God! Sono stanco morta!' I'm exhausted."

Business soared as more people learned of Carlino's. Many chefs in Philadelphia heard about the incredible homemade pasta Mama made and were regularly ordering it for their discriminating patrons. The pasta machine Mama had bought from Italy could not keep up with the volume. "We had to trade up for a bigger one," daughter-in-law Laura Carlino said.

Mama getting ready to be a star!

CHAPTER NINE

MAMA'S DREAM TO BE FIRST

Executive Pastry Chef Jessica Pachorkowsky-Perez places her palm on the metal counter in the bakery and says, "Mama rolled out her dough right here beside me." She is surrounded by bins of utensils, bowls from tiny to gargantuan, candies, sprinkles, and decorating tools.

Jessica shares her viewpoint on how the Carlinos established a unique place in the food business. "When Mama started the business, she did it to survive. It grew more than she ever dreamed.

Carlino's homemade pasta became the first in so many ways. Carlino's was a specialty market before there were specialty markets." Jessica continued with her comments, her tone serious. "Mama worked hard to create success. It seemed to me, she set it all up, got it to be where it needed to be, and then she said, 'Here,' and laid down to rest." Jessica pauses gathering her emotions. Then adds, "Her grandchildren were her life. She prepared them to carry on the business."

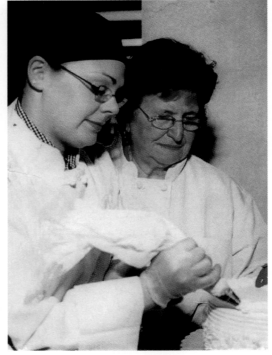

Tucking a wisp of dark hair under her cap, she walks over to a curving five-foot tall display shelf holding a huge selection of cookies. "Mama always wanted to be innovative. She was always on the alert for new ways to do things." Jessica points out a few of Mama's personal favorites: lemon anginetti cookies and bocconotti. It was Mama's dream to continue offering innovations in all departments."

Chef Jessica and Mama

Lemon Anginetti Cookies

INGREDIENTS:

FOR THE COOKIES

1 ¼ cups sugar
¾ cup milk
¾ cup vegetable oil
1 ¼ tablespoon baking powder
Flour, to texture

FOR THE FROSTING

3 cups confectioner's sugar
¼ cup water
¼ teaspoon lemon oil
½ teaspoon lemon zest

DIRECTIONS:

1. Preheat oven to 350°F.

2. Whip the eggs and the sugar on high with an electric mixer until the eggs triple in volume and mixture is very light and fluffy. Keep whipping until the yolks form ribbons when drizzled from the whisk.

3. Lower speed to medium and add the oil, milk, and vanilla while the yolks are still whipping.

4. Add the baking powder and about a cup of flour to form a very loose dough. The cookie dough should be very sticky.

5. Turn the dough out onto a floured surface and slowly knead in more flour until soft dough is formed.

   These cookies are very light and soft so it is very important not to overwork the dough.

6. Using a small cookie scoop, drop dough onto a slightly greased cookie sheet spacing them about 2 inches apart. Bake for about 10-12 minutes or until lightly browned around the edges.

7. Remove cookies from the cookie sheet and cool completely on wire cookie rack.

TO MAKE LEMON FROSTING

1. Combine confectioner's sugar, water, lemon zest, and lemon oil in a medium sized bowl and whisk until smooth.

2. Frost the tops of each cookie with a metal spatula and sprinkle with rainbow nonpareils.

Please make the following adjustment to the recipe on page 89

LEMON ANGINETTI COOKIES

Yield: 2 dozen | Time: 45 minutes

INGREDIENTS:

FOR THE COOKIES

4 eggs
1 ¼ cups sugar
¾ cup milk
¾ cup vegetable oil
1 tablespoon vanilla extract
1 ¼ tablespoons baking powder
Flour, to texture

Rainbow nonpareils, optional

FOR THE FROSTING

3 cups confectioner's sugar
¼ cup water
¼ teaspoon lemon oil
½ teaspoon lemon zest

DIRECTIONS:

1. Preheat oven to 350°F.
2. Whip the eggs and the sugar on high with an electric mixer until the eggs triple in volume and the mixture is very light and fluffy. Keep whipping until the mixture forms ribbons when drizzled from the whisk.
3. Lower speed to medium and add the oil, milk and vanilla while the egg mixture is still whipping.
4. Add the baking powder and about a cup of flour to form very loose dough. The cookie dough should be very sticky.
5. Turn the dough out onto a floured surface and slowly knead in more flour until soft dough is formed. *These cookies are very light and soft so it is very important not to overwork the dough.*
6. Using a small cookie scoop, drop dough onto a slightly greased cookie sheet spacing them about 2 inches apart. Bake for about 10-12 minutes or until lightly browned around the edges.
7. Remove cookies from the cookie sheet and cool completely on wire cookie rack.

TO MAKE LEMON FROSTING
1. Combine confectioner's sugar, water, lemon zest, and lemon oil in a medium sized bowl and whisk until smooth.
2. Frost the tops of each cookie with a metal spatula and sprinkle with rainbow nonpareils, if desired.

Lemon Anginetti Cookies

Bocconotti

~ Yield: 16 | Time: 1 ½ hours ~

**For this recipe you will need 16 petite fluted tartlet shell molds.*

INGREDIENTS:

PASTRY DOUGH

5 eggs
¼ cup sugar
¼ cup olive oil

½ lemon, zest only
Flour, to texture

FILLING

5 ounces almonds
3 tablespoons good quality cocoa powder
4 ounces good quality dark chocolate
½ cup sugar

½ teaspoon cinnamon
4 egg whites
1 teaspoon pure vanilla extract

DIRECTIONS:

DOUGH

1. Beat the eggs and the sugar with an electric mixer until very fluffy and ribbons form on top of mixture.

2. Slowly add the olive oil in a slow steady stream.

3. Add the zest, reduce the mixer speed to low, and switch to the paddle attachment.

4. Add flour slowly until a soft dough forms.

5. Turn the dough out onto a lightly floured surface, and knead it gently, just until it comes together into a ball.

6. Wrap the dough in plastic wrap and refrigerate for at least 1 hour.

7. Preheat the oven to 350° F.

Bocconotti

FILLING:

1. Beat the egg whites until stiff peaks form. Set aside.

2. Place all dry ingredients in a food processor and pulse until a course crumbly consistency is formed.

3. Gently fold the dry ingredients and the vanilla into the beaten egg whites half at a time.

4. Take a small amount to dough into your hands and roll into a tiny round.

5. Using your hands press the ball into a tartlet mold. Make sure to press the dough up the sides of the mold as well.

6. Trim off any extra dough.

7. Repeat steps 4-6 until all tartlet molds are filled.

8. Once all tartlet molds are ready place a heaping tablespoon of filling into each tartlet. Bake at 350 degrees for 12-15 minutes. Remove from oven and cool on wire rack. Once cool, remove bocconotti from molds and dust with powdered sugar.

ASSEMBLY:

1. Lightly grease the tartlet molds.

2. Take a small amount of dough into your hands and roll into a tiny ball.

3. Using your hands press the ball into a tartlet mold. Make sure to press the dough up the sides of the mold as well.

4. Trim off any extra dough.

5. Repeat steps until all tartlet molds are filled.

6. Once all tartlet molds are ready, place a heaping tablespoon of filling into each tartlet. Bake at 350° F 12-15 minutes, or until lightly browned. Remove from oven and cool on wire rack. Once cool, remove bocconotti from molds and dust with powdered sugar.

CHAPTER TEN

YOU LIVE AND DIE FOR THE WEDDINGS!

Pat Carlino came up with a brilliant idea for his daughter's wedding based on a tradition he remembers from his birthplace in Abruzzo, Italy. It was a way to honor the past, his mother, and bring a bit of fun to the present. Over dinner and drinks one evening with his soon-to-be son-in-law Joe, he asked with a half smile, "Are you going to serenade Angela?" Joe shook his head and dismissed the idea saying, "No, they don't do that anymore." Pat persisted, "It might be fun to honor the tradition. Think about it."

Joe did think about it, talked it over with his friends, and eventually acquiesced.

That was all Pat needed to hear and he sprang into action. Pat had serious business to attend to and no time to lose as the wedding rehearsal was approaching. He needed to search for the necessary ingredients for a surprise.

A few weeks later Angela and Joe's wedding rehearsal dinner was coming to a close. All enjoyed an abundance of lavish food and good spirits. As guests gathered to leave, the bride-to-be asked Joe to join her family for a small reunion back at the house. His response surprised her. Joe, a tall articulate young man, suddenly looked like a man with his hand stuck in the cookie jar. He said, "I think I'm going to hang with the guys tonight."

Angela rolled her dark eyes and said "WHAT?" But Joe stayed firm, saying, "I'm a little tired. You go ahead."

Shaking her head and smiling as she recalled the ladies' half of the story, Laura Carlino recounts, "Angela was NOT happy with Joe during the ride home. She couldn't believe he was not accompanying us home with all of the aunts and uncles who had come all the way from Italy for the wedding."

When they arrived home Laura asked Angela to show her the wedding shoes as she needed to check the straps. Laura describes clumping upstairs to Angela's bedroom on the second floor. "While I checked the straps, we heard a small tap at the window. Angela looked at me and asked, 'What's that?' I just made a face of surprise.

"A few seconds later we heard a bang! Something hit the window hard. Angela flashed over to the window, pushed the mini blinds aside, and shrieked, 'There's a bunch of people down there in our yard.' She lifted open the window and looked directly down at Joe, standing in the center of a pack of his friends, waving his arms at her with a hangdog grin.

"Uncle Vincenzo from Casoli, Italy, stood solidly next to Joe, mandolin at the ready in his strong but sensitive arms. Vincenzo ever so gently began strumming the instrument and Joe opened his mouth. His voice was somewhere between that of a twelve-year-old pubescent boy and a stray cat in heat. Angela gasped, dumbstruck. The none-too-melodious words lurched, 'You're just too good to be true . . . can't take my eyes off of you!'"

Shock turned to hysterics among the listeners as Joe proceeded to butcher the familiar tune. Angela understood why Joe had deserted her. All was forgiven.

As the old Italian ritual of serenading came to life under a white moon in the Carlinos' front yard, another tradition was being carried out in the backyard. Uncle Frank and Pat were working at a fevered pitch to make the customary feast. A mouth-watering roasting smell wafted across the yard. What was the delectable meat sizzling on the grill? Of course it was ram kabob! Pat had searched the countryside looking for this hard-to-find specialty meat. Only a few farmers will castrate and kill the ram in a humane fashion. It produces succulent, ultra-tender meat. As he relates the story, a smile spreads across his face. "If Mama were here, she would have been the first one in the kitchen to prepare it."

It's a tricky job to ready the meat for cooking. Uncle Frank uses a special box-like form made in Italy and covered with tiny holes. He holds the form in one hand and places a square chunk of meat into the box. Next he inserts wooden skewers into the holes. Then he takes a knife and slices through slots in the box. The result is perfectly shaped kabobs, ready for the grill. That night Frank grilled nearly 300 kabobs. The family relished every bite. The soon-to-be son-in-law and his non-Italian buddies raved about the succulent flavor.

According to Uncle Frank, there is great significance embedded in the tradition of serenading. He said, "In the old days, at nighttime a man may go to the house of a girl he knows. While playing his accordion he sings a song. If he plays two songs, the girl knows his intention is friendship. If he plays three to four songs, she knows he likes her and the family might put a light on and invite the man in. If he plays six songs," Uncle Frank pauses and lifts his wiry eyebrows, "he loves her. But does she love him back? Big question." The family usually invites him in for a drink and conversation to establish the nature of the relationship.

A medieval Roman song of unknown authorship describes the serenading process:

> *The suitor is asking for help,*
> *Shine forth your stars,*
> *Make it feel like spring.*
> *Assist the boy with his marriage plea.*

Papa Pat remembers yet another Italian wedding tradition. Typically the relatives take pains to find out where the couple will spend their wedding night. The following morning they go to the site. As they approach, they begin stomping their feet and they speak la forza. (loudly, in Italian) When they arrive at the newlyweds' room, they begin to bang ferociously at the door. Buongiorno! Get up you lazy people. A traditional early morning feast of spaghetti with olive oil and garlic quickly ensues.

In Angela and Joe's case the family decided to prepare this dish at about 3:00 in the morning, thus completing a 24-hour cycle of feasting, celebrating, singing, and dancing. The Carlinos love to entertain and have a good time while celebrating the cherished old-country ways.

PHANTOM OF THE HOPE CHEST

Traditions offer families a sense of continuity, reassurance, and a way to honor personal history. Mama held her traditions with fierce loyalty. Mama had a hope chest brought over from Italy and it held many traditional items from her country. In her case traditions offered her a way to plan for future events. Nick recalls, "Mom-mom made it clear. For a proper wedding you needed three items, a gorgeous wedding dress, flowers, and confetti (candy-coated almonds from Abruzzo). "What we didn't know," he says with half a smile, "she had a plan."

Mama had eloped and had no wedding so she missed the delicious, creative sense of planning for a wedding, with all the menus, dresses, and themes, all glorious happenings in her mind. Weddings were an important theme for Mama; she fashioned a crystal ball of vision for the wedding of her granddaughter Angela.

*Mama's granddaughter, Angela,
on her wedding day– 2010*

When Mama left Italy she packed up her clothes and personal items and placed them lovingly into her hope chest. Constructed of metal and hand painted blue and gold, it was a safe container for the long transport. When it landed in her home she set it aside, still holding hand-crocheted linens and tablemats made by her grandmother. On trips she would usually bring back items to go into the chest and she talked to Angela about the importance.

Angela had many conversations with Mama about the all-important day and other issues as well. Angela's eyes, golden-brown, crinkle up as she pulls her long brilliantly thick hair to the side and says matter-of-factly, "Mama had wise words for me." She pauses thoughtfully and then recites the wisdom, "Be the strongest you can be, do things on your own, be a respectful woman, and don't wait for some man."

Another declaration Angela often heard from Mama was, "If you are a good girl, when you get married I'm going to buy you a dress like Princess Diana!" Angela dreamed and Mama dreamed. And the day came when Angela met an extraordinary man and she happily brought him home to meet the family.

Pat's face breaks into a dimpled grin and his eyes glisten with emotion as he recalls his mother's keen intuitive sense in assessing romantic attraction. "The first time Angela brought Joe over, Mama sized him up very quickly. She liked him and as soon as the couple left, Mama with a knowing look, said, 'I see it in their eyes. He's the one.' She was sure they would wed. And in the same breath she would worry, 'I hope I make it to the wedding.'"

Sadly, Mama would not be there when it came time to pick out the dress for her wedding but Angela insisted her dad come to the store and help with the final choice. As Angela appeared from behind a curtained booth, Pat witnessed his glowing daughter modeling a voluminous, sparkling white wedding gown and he quickly declared, "That's it!" He knew Mama would have loved this particular dress. Paradoxically, her presence arose in an uncanny fashion about a week before the wedding.

Laura and Angela climbed the stairs to the attic on a mission to find "something old" for Angela to wear. As they carefully lifted the squeaky metal lid of the hope chest, the aroma of starch and spice greeted their senses. The container was filled to the brim. Settling on the floor beside the hope chest, they took turns lifting out items. In the dim light they noticed a folded envelope wedged between layers of tissue paper. Laura opened the envelope and in astonishment discovered a wad of cash. Tens and twenties and singles, obviously gathered over time, were stowed away.

Joe and Angela Milani on their wedding day

Mother and daughter turned to each other, tears spilling. Joy and sadness mixed like a bouquet of bright sunny flowers and subdued foliage. Later that evening Pat heard news of the find. He knew instantly that the money was for the Diana dress! He knew without a doubt that his thoughtful mother had made sure the proper traditions would be sustained.

Angela Carlino, Mama's granddaughter, dressed in a gown billowing with folds of white satin and sparkling crystals, prepares to enter center stage. This day would be remembered as a grand Italian wedding. After the wedding service Angela and her groom Joe Milani swoosh into the dining room at the Union League in Philadelphia for the reception. A surprise awaits them. Mama's handmade biscotti has been unearthed from the deep freezer and lies on a side dish by the bride and groom's place setting.

Biscotti di Prato

❧ Yield: Approx. 3 dozen | Time: 1 hour ❧

INGREDIENTS:

5 whole eggs + 5 yolks
4 cups sugar
5 cups flour
1 ½ cups whole almonds,
slightly toasted
Zest of ½ an orange
½ teaspoon pure vanilla extract

DIRECTIONS:

1. Preheat oven at 350°F.

2. Beat the eggs, yolks, and sugar on high with an electric mixer until they are a pale color and smooth. Keep beating until the yolks form ribbons when drizzled from the whisk.

3. Lower speed to medium and slowly add the flour, almonds, orange zest, and vanilla until combined.

4. Turn mixture out onto table and form 2 long logs that are about 1 inch high and about 1 ½ inches wide.

5. Lay logs on a greased baking sheet and set aside for 30 minutes.

6. Brush the loaves with egg whites.

7. Bake for 15 minutes or until risen and firm.

8. Remove from oven and slice ½ inch wide diagonal slices using a serrated knife.

9. Return to oven and toast until lightly golden.

These cookies are passed down from Mama's great aunt Rosetta from Florence. These are authentic Florentine biscotti traditionally served with Vin santo.

Spaghetti Aglio e Olio

(Spaghetti with Oil and Garlic)

Serves: 4-6 | Time: 20 minutes

INGREDIENTS:

½ - ¾ cup Extra Virgin Olive Oil,
   plus more for drizzling
6 garlic cloves, peeled and thinly sliced
½ teaspoon red pepper flakes
1 small can anchovies in olive oil
½ teaspoon salt

½ lemon
Large handful chopped Italian parsley
1 pound dried spaghetti
1 cup grated Parmigiano Reggiano,
   optional

DIRECTIONS:

1. Heat the olive oil slowly with the garlic in a small skillet. When the garlic turns opaque, add the red pepper flakes, anchovies, the salt, and squeeze the lemon into the hot oil.

2. Turn off the heat and let the garlic turn light golden at the edges. The garlic will continue to cook in the hot oil. When the oil has cooled somewhat, add the parsley.

3. In the meantime, bring 6 quarts water to a rolling boil, add salt, and cook spaghetti until al dente.

4. Drain the pasta well in a colander and place in a shallow serving bowl.

5. Pour the warm olive oil sauce over the pasta and mix well.

6. If desired, drizzle more Extra Virgin Olive Oil and Parmigiano Reggiano on top. Stir and serve immediately.

Arrosticini

(Skewered Marinated Lamb)

* Served at Angela's Serenade. Prepared by Uncle Frank and John DiMichele.

⤳ Serves: 4 | Time: 45 minutes ⤳

INGREDIENTS:

½ pound deboned lamb shoulder
1 garlic clove
2 tablespoons Extra Virgin Olive Oil
Salt

Fresh ground black pepper
½ teaspoon dried rosemary
12 small skewers, soaked in water

DIRECTIONS:

1. Slice the meat into strips about ½ inch wide and 2 inches long. Do not trim away the fat, but try to have lean meat attached to some fat in as many pieces as possible. The fat will melt partly in the cooking, fueling the fire, and sweetening the meat.

2. Mash the garlic with a heavy knife handle, crushing it enough to split it and loosen the peel, which will be removed and discarded.

3. Put the meat in a bowl, adding the oil, salt, ground black pepper to taste, rosemary, and garlic. Toss well, thoroughly coating the meat. Let the lamb marinate in the refrigerator for 4 to 6 hours. Turn the lamb pieces from time to time.

4. Take the meat out at least 30 minutes before cooking.

5. Light the charcoal or prepare a wooden fire.

6. Turn the meat thoroughly one more time, and then skewer it, piercing each strip in at least two places.

7. When the fire is hot, place the skewers as close as possible to the source of heat. Cook for 3 minutes on one side, then turn the skewers and cook for 2 to 3 minutes on the other. A small, thin crust should form on all sides of the meat. Serve immediately.

Chef Jessica had prophetically stowed the precious cookies (saved from the opening of the new store) in the sub-zero freezer. She knew the crisp texture would defrost back into perfection. When Angela sits down and notices her grandmother's handiwork she cannot hold back the tears. "Mama is still with me!" she cries.

Heart storming: using your heart rather than your head
as a source of opportunity for creation.
~ playing on the radio

Mama bent over the table, knife in hand, slicing the dough into perfect portions. Her short hair, curled on her forehead hid perspiration as she proceeded with her task. She'd been making biscotti for weeks. Though her family pleaded with her to slow down. She would have none of it.

"I make enough for friends," she said adamantly.

Indeed it was a tough bill to fill. Mama had been making friends for more than thirty years, first in her home in Ardmore, then in Carlino's Homemade Pasta, and at numerous farmers markets in the area. Friends and patrons numbered in the thousands. The whole family had been preparing for the grand opening of the new Carlino's Market in West Chester just days away.

The smell of toasted almonds hung in the air as biscotti piled up on all the counter tops. Executive Chef Jessica Perez asked why it was so important to have such large amounts. Mama told her in no uncertain terms, "I want every person who comes in to have biscotti as a gift from me."

A typical generous gesture from Mama Carlino, Jessica knew from experience there would be no stopping her. As Chef Luigi likes to say, "Once she gets an idea in her head, she's like a freight train." Jessica stepped in and assisted, carrying the heavy trays to the ovens, taking the finished biscotti out and letting them cool, and lastly packaging each pastry in a shimmering wrapper.

Joe and Angela cut their
9-tier wedding cake
created by Carlino's pastry chefs

The Carlino family at Mama and Nicola's 50th Anniversary party- 2005

Chapter Eleven

Life Lessons

Mama's Cucina

Nick traces back his first memories of the family's store in Ardmore. It was a place of hard work and joy, and a place where Nick and his sister spent many hours in Mama's company. "I was about four and my sister was six when the school bus dropped us off a block away from the store. Mom-mom would be waiting, wearing her white apron. After a big hug and kiss, we each held her hand as we walked the short block to the store. Sandwiches awaited us: a proscuitto sandwich for me and mortadella for Angela."

Laura recalls Angela's favorite snack. "Mama poured fresh sauce into a cup, and Angela would tear off a piece of rustic bread and dip bread into the sauce. No candy bars for her!" Mama's favorite joke from that time was, "Little Angela with her skinny legs . . . I am a good cook but she doesn't fatten up." Laura delights in recalling the early days. "Angela was a happy little girl with Shirley Temple curls flecked with gold. With a dimple in one cheek and an agile smile she'd ask, brown eyes twinkling, 'Nonna, where is the sauce?'"

Nick continues, "After our snack, Angela would go straight to the kitchen to help cook while I wandered around the store making friends and helping customers." Young, old, Italian, French, Polish, Jewish all were welcomed at Carlino's. The store was more than a business; it was an extended caring family. Knowing customers' lives, who is getting married, who was sick, and who graduated were all part of the personal touch that helped make a business successful. Mama never stopped working to meet the needs of her family. To Nick, Mama was a warm bulb radiating exuberance and love.

While customers were, in some ways, extended family, family sometimes acted as customers. The nightly meal was often a taste-testing experiment. A consummate innovator, Mama would present her latest culinary efforts, followed by a quiz as to what exactly we liked or didn't like about a dish. If the chicken cacciatore met with

Nick and Angela Carlino - 1993

family approval, it would appear in the store the following day. Less successful dishes would return at a later meal in a new guise for a revised assessment. Pretty good was never acceptable to Mama.

Angela laughs recalling one of Mama's observations, "You can tell if someone is a dirty cook – just look at her apron!" Nick always admired Mama's intuition. "She had feelings about people, she knew whom she could trust and who valued her recipes."

In regards to how she felt about wealth she'd say, "I don't want to be a millionaire, I just want enough money so I can buy something without having to think about it twice."

Nick says, "Her training methods were very clear cut. If she was not happy with an action or preparation style, you'd get the look, the look of death!"

HOLIDAY SOUP STORY

Her mind was made up; she must go to Italy and bring back a critical piece of equipment. Nick and Angela would go with Mama to watch her make a deal.

Speaking in rapid flowing Italian, she discussed the negotiations with her cousin, Giuseppe Travaglini. Nick quips, "She wanted to end meatball duty. That was when all 13 of us lined up to make the meatballs by hand." The new freedom machine was a smaller version of the regular meatball machine they had purchased years ago. The new machine would make tiny meatballs. With her cousin's help, she was able to acquire a highly specialized machine. Negotiations had stalled and Mama traveled to Italy to move them forward. Nick recalls, "I learned a lot by observing Mama's drive to finish the deal."

The first machine of its kind, it needed to be adapted to U.S. standards. It took six months for the machine to arrive due to all the regulations. After months of intense communication the prize machine was delivered and the Carlinos became the first in the world to have this type of machine. Nick notes a gold stamp on the back as proof.

Once it was set up, Mama and chefs worked tirelessly to get the machine working properly. At last, with the equipment in place Mama was able to make the wildly popular Italian wedding soup, also known as holiday soup, in large amounts. The meatballs are also used in lasagnas.

Mama's Holiday Soup

❧ Serves: 8-10 | Time: 2 ½ hours, including prep time for mini meatballs ❧

INGREDIENTS:

1 (3-4 pound) stewing chicken, cut in
   quarters and thoroughly rinsed
1 large onion, peeled and cut in half
4 celery stalks, cut in half
3 carrots, peeled and cut in half
1 head escarole, green leaves only,
   washed and thoroughly chopped

Mini Meatballs, 1 batch,
   (recipe on page 83)
¾ pound pastina (small pasta), cooked
   according to package directions
2 tablespoons kosher salt, additional salt,
   to taste
Ground black pepper, to taste
Scrippelle, 1 batch, *(recipe on page 111)*

DIRECTIONS:

1. In a large stock pot, add chicken, onions, celery, carrots and salt.

2. Add enough water to cover 2 inches above the ingredients to allow everything to boil freely.

3. Simmer, uncovered, until the chicken begins to come off the bone (about 1 ½ hours). Occasionally skim off the foam from the top.

4. Remove chicken from the broth and strain vegetables, add to separate bowls to cool.

5. When chicken is cool enough to handle, shred by hand, discarding the skin and bones.

6. Dice all of the cooked vegetables.

7. Replace the broth back into stock pot.

8. Add escarole, shredded chicken, mini meatballs, and cooked vegetables.

9. Bring the soup to a boil and continue to boil for 5 minutes.

10. Season with salt and pepper.

11. Add cooked pasta.

12. Ladle soup into individual bowls (being sure to include the mini meatballs to each dish). Add a small handful of scrippelle, if desired.

(This is one of Laura Carlino's favorites.)

Mama's Holiday Soup

SCRIPPELLE

(Crepes used to top off Holiday Soup)

∽ Serves: 8-10 | Time: 30 minutes ∽

INGREDIENTS:

4 eggs, cracked
4 tablespoons milk
2 tablespoons flour

¼ cup grated Parmigiano
   Reggiano cheese
Salt to taste
Extra Virgin Olive Oil

DIRECTIONS:

1. In a mixing bowl, combine all ingredients and whisk by hand.

2. Heat a small, 6 inch, non-stick pan.

3. Carefully and lightly rub a paper towel dipped in olive oil over the pan's surface.

4. Once the pan is hot, pour about ¼ cup batter into the pan and swirl so that the batter makes a thin layer.

5. Make sure crepe is not sticking by lifting one corner.

6. Cook very lightly; and flip over gently.

7. Lightly cook the other side until batter is no longer wet.

8. Once crepe is done on both sides, flip onto a work surface and let cool completely.

9. Continue cooking batter until it is all used up.

10. Once crepes are cooled, stack them, cover with plastic wrap and refrigerate for up to 1 week or freeze for up to 3 months.

11. When you are ready to use the crepes in the holiday soup; roll one at a time, and using a sharp knife, cut into thin strips, creating ribbons.

12. Sprinkle on top of hot soup.

The Proper Way to Prepare Fish

"La puzza," the stench, did not stop seven-year-old Angela from having fun with fish, even if the fish's eyeballs occasionally fell out and rolled around on the floor like tiny marbles. It was all part of the ritual.

Nicola and Pat did not have far to go to find abundant trout fishing. Their favorite spot was right in Havertown and success was easy. The stream was loaded. They'd come back with heaping buckets full of fish. As soon as the men came in, Mama would call for Angela. "Come, we have to clean all these damn fish!" It was one difficult, painstaking project but Angela was an apt student. Mama patiently showed her how to cut the fins off with scissors, save the head and carefully remove the entrails.

Carmen preparing the freshly caught trout

Fish is an important part of the family's diet and Angela learned early on the proper way to prepare fish. Old-school preparation was simple: season the fish with olive oil, lemon, and fresh rosemary, then wrap each fish in aluminum foil and bake in the oven. Angela explains, "At dinner we each had our own packet to unwrap and Grandpop (an expert at filleting fish) showed us how to fillet or debone the trout. It was delicious."

Now Angela is the one to come up with recipes using fish.

Angela's Whole Fresh Trout Baked in Foil

⁓ Serves: 4 | Time: 25 minutes ⁓

INGREDIENTS:

4 whole small trout
  (Brook or Rainbow preferred), boned
Extra Virgin Olive Oil
3 lemons, sliced into thin rounds

8 sprigs fresh rosemary
8 sprigs fresh Italian flat leaf parsley
4 cloves garlic, finely chopped
Salt and Pepper, to taste

DIRECTIONS:

1. Preheat oven to 450°F. Cut four sheets of heavy duty aluminum foil into squares that are three inches longer than your fish. Oil the dull side of the foil with olive oil, and place a trout on each square.

2. Season both sides with salt and pepper, and open them out flat. Place 2 sprigs each of parsley and rosemary and 3 slices of lemon in the cavity of each fish. Sprinkle with a quarter of the chopped garlic. Fold fish back together. Drizzle ½ teaspoon olive oil over each fish and carefully coat each side without flipping the fish over.

3. Making sure that the trout are in the middle of each square; fold up the foil loosely, grabbing at the edges and crimping together tightly to make a packet.

4. Place on a baking sheet and bake for 15-20 minutes, checking at 15 minutes. Check the fish by piercing with a fork and the fish meat flakes.

5. To serve, place one foil packet on each plate, and either serve fish in the packet to keep the juices contained, or remove the fish from the foil and top fish with the juices remaining in the foil packet.

Angela's Whole Fresh Trout Baked in Foil

Philip and Nonna Santa DiNardo, Laura's mom

Summer Fresh Tomatoes

Summer offers a time for the Carlinos to continue a few traditions from the old country. Philip perks up on the topic of "SAUCE." With a slight flicker in his eyes he says, "Spaghetti and sauce -- my number one favorite food." He recalls harvesting the robust tomato crop, astutely planted and maintained by Nicola just steps away from the house in the backyard.

When Mama or Nicola deemed the tomatoes to be at peak ripeness, the children pulled the plump, red tomatoes off the plants, smelling the green stems, the scent of summer.

Santa DiNardo, Laura's mother, and Philip were in charge of dousing the tomatoes in hot water for a couple of minutes. Then with a slotted spoon he would lift them out and place them in cold water. After cooling, they would carefully peel off the skins. Then it was time for pippare, a slow, low heat, which turns the tomatoes into a luscious luminous sauce.

"Adding fresh whole basil leaves," Philip says, "is the final step for the sauce." The smile of the boy within slides across his face as he adds, "Mama would add a little more to my plate saying, 'A little more won't hurt. You need to eat well to grow!'"

Master sauce maker Uncle Frank recalls the old way (his grandmother's way) of making sauce on the family's farm. "The tomatoes we planted were different, small and tougher, more the size of a large walnut. They did not receive as much water. My grandmother had to cook the tomatoes longer to turn them into sauce. These days the tomatoes we use in our sauce are softer; we simmer them for no longer than two hours. If you cook them too long, they get sour tasting."

Insalata Panzanella

(Bread Salad)

❧ Serves: 6 | Time: 20 minutes ❧

INGREDIENTS:

1 large loaf, day-old crusty Italian bread, crusts removed and cut into ½-inch cubes

4 ripe tomatoes, cored, seeded, and cut into ½-inch cubes

1 cup red onion, diced

3 tablespoons red wine vinegar

2 cloves garlic, minced

5 tablespoons extra virgin olive oil

Salt and Pepper to taste

1 cup sharp Asiago cheese, shaved

14 fresh basil leaves, shredded by hand, plus more for garnishing

DIRECTIONS:

1. In a large bowl, toss the bread, tomatoes, onions, and shredded basil leaves together until well mixed.

2. In a small mixing bowl, whisk together vinegar, garlic, salt and pepper.

3. While whisking vigorously, add the olive oil in a slow, steady stream allowing the vinaigrette to form an emulsion.

4. Let sit for 15 minutes before serving to allow the bread to soak up the juices.

5. Add shaved Asiago cheese. Mix.

6. Decorate with fresh basil leaves.

Italy, 1960, outside of Mama's house where she stewed the summer crop of tomatoes

Pomodori Fritti

(Polenta-Encrusted Tomato Slices)

≈ Serves 4-6 | Time: 20-30 minutes ≈

INGREDIENTS:

4-6 red, ripe, yet firm tomatoes
½ cup coarse polenta or yellow cornmeal
Coarse salt and freshly ground black pepper to taste
¼ cup Extra Virgin Olive Oil
Aged Balsamic Vinegar, to drizzle
10 fresh basil leaves

DIRECTIONS:

1. Cut a thin slice from the stem end of each tomato and discard. Cut tomatoes into ½-inch thick slices. Place the cornmeal in a shallow bowl or plate and add salt and pepper to taste. Start heating the olive oil in a large skillet.

2. Meanwhile, lightly dredge the tomato slices in the seasoned cornmeal. When the oil is very hot, carefully place the tomato slices in the skillet, being careful not to crowd them. Every minute or so gently nudge the tomato slices with a spatula to prevent them from sticking. If the pan is hot enough, the tomato slices will be easy to turn over as soon as the cornmeal coating is properly cooked. It should be nice and crunchy.

3. Turn over the slices and fry them on the other side. Immediately remove the tomato slices from the skillet and arrange them on a serving platter. Drizzle some aged balsamic vinegar over the tomatoes. Stack the basil leaves and roll them. Holding the basil roll carefully cut it crosswise into thin strips. Sprinkle the basil over the tomatoes.

Linguine al Tonno alla Puttanesca

(Linguine with Fresh Tuna Puttanesca Style)

❧ Serves: 4-6 | Time: 30 minutes ❧

INGREDIENTS:

¼ cup Extra Virgin Olive Oil
4-5 garlic cloves, peeled and minced
½- 1 teaspoon red chili pepper flakes
12 Roma tomatoes, peeled, seeded,
   chopped
1 tablespoon capers
¼ cup pitted Kalamata Olives,
   cut into quarters lengthwise
3 anchovy fillets, rinsed in cold water
   and finely chopped.
1 pound fresh tuna, cut roughly into 1-inch dice
1 pound linguine pasta
2 tablespoons Kosher Salt (for pasta water)
Pepperoncini Infused Extra Virgin Olive Oil (optional)

DIRECTIONS:

1. Heat the olive oil in a skillet over moderate heat. Add the garlic and red chili
    pepper flakes and let cook just until the garlic begins to give off its characteristic
    fragrance. Add the tomatoes and cook over high heat, stirring frequently until
    tomatoes begin to break down and give off their juice.

2. Add the capers and olives, turn down heat, and continue to cook until the sauce
    begins to thicken. Add the anchovies and tuna. Simmer until the tuna is cooked
    through and the sauce thickens.

3. Meanwhile, cook the linguine in 6 quarts boiling salted water until al dente.
    Drain the pasta in a colander, and then add the drained pasta to the skillet with
    the tomato-tuna sauce. Toss the linguine with the sauce over high heat so that the
    pasta begins to absorb some of the sauce. Place the pasta immediately in a large
    shallow serving bowl.

4. Drizzle Pepperoncini Infused Extra Virgin Olive Oil for added flavor.

Spaghetti alla Carbonara

❧ Serves 4-6 | Time: 50 minutes ❧

INGREDIENTS:

4 slices pancetta (Italian Bacon)
4 egg yolks
⅛ teaspoon hot red pepper flakes
¼ cup heavy cream
½ cup freshly grated Pecorino Romano Cheese, to mix with eggs
1 pound fresh spaghetti
2 tablespoons kosher salt (for pasta water)
2 tablespoons butter, melted
¼ cup freshly grated Pecorino Romano Cheese, to top spaghetti

DIRECTIONS:

1. In a medium skillet, fry pancetta over medium-low heat until crisp. Drain. Crumble pancetta. Set aside.

2. In a large mixing bowl, beat egg yolks and hot red pepper flakes. Stir in cream and ½ cup Pecorino Romano. Set aside.

3. Bring 6 quarts water to a rolling boil, add salt, and cook spaghetti until al dente. Drain in colander. Return to saucepan. Add egg mixture, pancetta and butter. Cook over medium-low heat until egg is set, stirring constantly. Serve immediately, adding the remaining Pecorino Romano to each serving dish.

For a more substantial dish, Mama would sauté ½ to ¾ cup of mushrooms with chopped shallots for 3-4 minutes then add to the pasta at Step 3.

Spaghetti alla Carbonara

STUFFED ARTICHOKES

Serves: 6 | Time: 45 minutes

INGREDIENTS:

6 medium artichokes, stems trimmed and choke removed
   *be sure to trim the dark green skin from the stem and the base of each artichoke.
3-4 lemons, halved
⅓ cup coarse breadcrumbs
½ cup Extra Virgin Olive Oil, plus more for drizzling
4-5 sprigs Italian flat leaf parsley, chopped
½ cup ricotta cheese
1 cup grated Pecorino Romano (preferably Locatelli)
½ teaspoon ground nutmeg
Kosher salt

DIRECTIONS:

1. Add cold water to a large bowl and add the juice of 2 lemons to it.

2. Continue to prepare each artichoke by cutting the upper ¾ inches off the tip of the entire artichoke. Once completed squeeze lemon juice over the entire artichoke and submerge in the acidic water bowl to keep from oxidizing.

3. Preheat the oven to 350°F.

4. In a separate large bowl, combine the bread crumbs, olive oil, parsley, cheeses and nutmeg. Stir thoroughly.

5. Season the mixture with salt and pepper to taste.

6. Remove the artichokes from the lemon water and pat dry. Place the artichokes on a separate platter and season with salt and drizzle with olive oil.

7. Taking one at a time, stuff each artichoke with the cheese and breadcrumb mixture being sure to fill between every petal. Place on a baking pan or dish (preferably with higher edges to contain the moisture). Continue until every artichoke is stuffed.

8. Sprinkle the remaining cheese and breadcrumb mixture over the tops of the artichokes.

9. Add about ¼ inch of water to the bottom of the baking pan to prevent scorching or burning.

10. Cover the pan with foil and place into the preheated oven.

11. Bake artichokes for 40 minutes. Carefully remove the foil and place the baking pan or dish under the broiler for 8-10 minutes to create a golden crust.

Stuffed Artichoke

Penne alla Vodka

❧ Serves: 4-6 | Time: 20 minutes ❧

INGREDIENTS:

⅔ cup Vodka
3 plum tomatoes, seeded and chopped
Pinch crushed red pepper
6 tablespoons butter
¾ cup whipping cream
½ cup freshly grated Parmigiano Reggiano cheese
1 pound penne pasta
2 tablespoons kosher salt (for pasta water)

DIRECTIONS:

1. In a large pot bring 6 quarts of water to a rolling boil and add salt.

2. Cook the pasta until al dente (firm to the bite).

3. Meanwhile, in a large skillet over medium heat, melt the butter. Add tomatoes and cook for 3 minutes, stirring frequently.

4. Add vodka and whipping cream; bring to a light boil until about half of the liquid has evaporated. Be sure to keep stirring as to not burn the cream.

5. Stir in crushed pepper flakes and simmer for an additional 2-3 minutes.

6. Remove from heat, and let stand for 2 minutes. Stir in the cheese until melted.

7. Add cooked penne to skillet. Toss until pasta is coated.

8. Serve immediately.

Penne alla Vodka

Bucantini All'Amarticiana

⤜ Serves 4 | Prep time: 25 minutes ⤛

INGREDIENTS:

6 slices pancetta (Italian bacon)
3 cloves garlic, cut in halves
1 small red onion, sliced thinly
2 teaspoons pepperoncini (red hot
   pepper flakes), or to taste
Salt and pepper, to taste

2 cups Basic Tomato Sauce *(recipe on page 81)*
1 pound bucatini pasta
2-3 sprigs Italian flat leaf parsley,
   roughly chopped
Locatelli or Pecorino Romano,
   freshly grated

DIRECTIONS:

1. Bring 6 quarts water to a rolling boil and add salt.

2. Lay the pancetta in a large frying pan over medium heat and fry until crisp.

3. Place the pancetta on a paper towel-lined plate and drain ⅓ of the fat from the frying pan.

4. When the pancetta is cool enough to handle, roughly chop and add back to the pan.

5. Over medium high heat, add the garlic, onion and pepperoncini to the pan, and cook for 6-8 minutes longer, or until the garlic is just browned and the onion softens.

6. Add the tomato sauce and season with salt and pepper, reduce the heat and simmer for 10-15 minutes.

7. While the sauce is simmering, add bucatini to the boiling water, and cook until al dente (firm to the bite).

8. Drain the pasta and add to the prepared sauce.

9. Sprinkle with fresh parsley and cheese. Serve immediately.

Zucchini con Fontina and Mozzarella

(Zucchini with Fontina and Mozzarella Cheese)

✎ Serves: 4 | Time: 1 hour ✎

INGREDIENTS:

6 to 8 ripe tomatoes
2 cloves garlic, minced
4 tablespoons Extra Virgin Olive Oil
10 fresh basil leaves, chopped
2 teaspoons dried basil leaves
¼ teaspoon salt
⅛ teaspoon black pepper
Oil for frying
3 medium zucchini, peeled and cut lengthwise into ¼ - inch slices
1 cup shredded Fontina (about 4 ounces)
1 cup shredded Mozzarella (about 4 ounces)

DIRECTIONS:

1. To remove peel from tomatoes: Place tomatoes in boiling water for 30 to 60 seconds. Remove from water. Plunge tomatoes into cold water. Remove and discard peel and seeds.

2. Chop the peeled tomatoes.

3. In large skillet, sauté garlic in olive oil.

4. Add tomatoes, basil, salt and pepper. Stir and cook until sauce thickens, 20 to 30 minutes.

5. Meanwhile, in medium skillet, heat ¼ inch vegetable oil over medium heat. Fry zucchini until golden brown, turning once. Drain on paper towels and allow zucchini to cool.

6. Preheat oven to 350°F.

7. Arrange half the zucchini in a 9-inch square baking dish. Cover with half the tomato sauce. Sprinkle with half the Fontina and half the mozzarella.

8. Repeat layers.

9. Bake until cheese melts, about 15 minutes. Serve immediately by cutting into squares as you would a traditional lasagna.

Zia Maria's Pasta con Proscuitto e Piselli

*Mama and her family loved sister-in-law, Maria's pasta with prosciutto and peas recipe! It is the perfect meal for a cold winter's night, or any night at all, really!

❧ Serves: 4 | Prep Time: 45 minutes ❧

INGREDIENTS:

1 pound Conchiglie Rigate Pasta
   (Shell-Shaped Pasta)
¼ cup Extra Virgin Olive Oil
¼ pound prosciutto (cut into cubes, approx.
   ¼ inch thick)
¼ pound ham (cut into cubes, approx.
   ¼ inch thick)
½ chicken breast (cut into cubes, approx.
   ¼ inch thick)

¼ Red Bell Pepper, seeded and cut into
   thin strips
¼ Green Bell Pepper, seeded and cut
   into thin strips
¼ Yellow Bell Pepper, seeded and cut
   into thin strips
3 Garlic Cloves
1 stalk celery, small dice
1 sprig Italian flat leaf parsley
½ pound porcini mushrooms, rough chop

DIRECTIONS:

1. In a large skillet, heat ¼ cup of olive oil over medium heat.

2. Add in the celery, red, green, and yellow peppers and sauté for 1 minute. After 1 minute add in the garlic cloves and parsley.

3. Add in the chicken and cook until lightly brown.

4. Add in prosciutto and ham. Let cook for 15 minutes and then add in the porcini mushrooms.

5. Cook all ingredients together for about 25 minutes, stirring occasionally

6. Meanwhile, in a large pot of boiling water, cook shell pasta until al dente. Drain.

7. Add the cooked pasta into the pot and mix all of the ingredients together.

8. Place in a large serving bowl. Serve immediately.

**Zia Maria's Tip: Sprinkle chopped parsley and a handful of Locatelli cheese
on top of your dish for some added flavor!*

Zia Maria' Pasta con Prosciutto e Piselli

Risotto alla Campagnola

(Country Style Risotto)

∽ Serves: 4-6 | Time: 30 minutes ∽

INGREDIENTS:

2 tablespoons Extra Virgin Olive Oil
½ onion, peeled and finely chopped
2 carrots, trimmed and finely chopped
2 celery stalks, trimmed and finely chopped
Handful coarsely chopped Italian flat leaf parsley, divided
2 cups Arborio rice
⅓ cup dry white wine
6 cups chicken broth
Salt to taste
6 ounces ricotta
2 tablespoons unsalted butter
½ cup grated Parmigiano Reggiano Cheese

DIRECTIONS:

1. Heat the olive oil in a large saucepan.

2. Add the onion, carrots, celery, and half the parsley, and cook slowly over low heat until the vegetables are wilted and nearly tender.

3. Add the rice and, stirring constantly, sauté until rice grains are opaque, approximately 1 to 2 minutes.

4. Meanwhile, heat the broth until it is very hot. Turn off the heat, but keep the broth hot on a warm burner. Add the white wine to the rice and cook slowly, stirring constantly, until it is completely absorbed. Add the hot broth to the rice one ladleful at a time, stirring frequently. The rice should cook very slowly over low heat. Wait until all the liquid is absorbed before adding the next ladleful of broth. Midway through the cooking time, add salt to taste.

5. When the risotto is just tender, add the ricotta, 2 tablespoons of butter, Parmigiano Reggiano Cheese, and the remaining parsley. Turn off the heat and stir vigorously until all the butter and cheese are absorbed and the ricotta is well mixed into the risotto. Serve immediately.

POLENTA WITH GORGONZOLA

～ Serves: 4 | Time: 1 hour, 15 minutes ～

INGREDIENTS:

4 cups water
½ teaspoon kosher salt
2 cups yellow cornmeal

7 ounces Gorgonzola cheese, thinly sliced
¼ pound fully cooked ham, sliced
butter, to grease

DIRECTIONS:

1. In a large stock pot, heat water and salt to boiling.

2. Add cornmeal, ½ cup at a time, stirring constantly with whisk to prevent lumps.

3. Cook over medium heat, stirring constantly until the polenta is very thick and has the consistency of thick mashed potatoes, 30 to 45 minutes.

   When the polenta begins to stiffen be sure to start using a wooden spoon for the rest of the cooking process.

4. Pour into 2-quart serving dish and pack down gently. Let cool.

5. Preheat oven to 350°F.

6. Butter 9-inch square baking dish. Set aside.

7. Cut polenta into ¼-inch slices. Arrange half the polenta, a third of the Gorgonzola and half the ham in prepared baking dish. Repeat layers. Top with remaining cheese.

8. Bake until cheese melts, 15 to 20 minutes. Serve immediately.

Making pastry . . .

Mama surrounded by delicious Carlino hearth-baked breads

Chapter Twelve

Holiday Chaos

Carlinos in Overdrive

In Italy many holidays combine rustic traditions, traditional cultural rites, and a spiritual context. Christmas may have originated in Italy; the red, white and green colors are the same as the national flag. Saint Francis of Assisi wrote and introduced "carols," composing them in Italian. Common throughout Italy are Christmas sweets, often made with nuts or almonds. Two popular traditional sweets are cicerchiata (honey balls), which Mama made, and spumetti.

Mama took her role in providing countless families with traditional foods seriously. Like the top of a wedding cake, holidays were a special crowning glory for Mama. Discovering a new gear, she'd shift up, release her memories, and approach the counter ready for countless hours of kneading, rolling, and crimping.

Pastry Chef Jessica says, "The holidays are pretty much around-the-clock baking." With her eyes flashing she recalls, "Mama would say '60 eggs' which meant a huge recipe was planned." A recipe she always helped with for Christmas was fried Italian Christmas cookies called calginetti. "Mama used ground chestnuts, marmalades, chocolate, espresso, and anything else she would want to throw in. We'd put all the ingredients in and Mama would taste it a million times. It sounds like an odd mixture, but somehow when it came out of the oven, it worked. Mama made 250 pounds a year almost by herself. Her comment each year was 'betta than alast year.'"

Laura recalls Mama saying at Easter time, "Oh, my arms ache." And Laura would ask, "How many loaves of Easter bread did you make?" Over the entire Easter season the number was approximately 2,000. The sweet raisin bread flavored with lemon and fondant icing was and is wildly popular. Mama loved lemon! She created many dishes with zesty lemon.

Nick loves recalling the local holiday stories. Some long-time customers tell them to each other. Every holiday the historic line of customers begins and quickly grows, wrapping its tail around the building. Customers stamp their feet like impatient horses at feeding time. Mama would instruct the chefs to make everything ready a half hour before opening time. Nick explains, "She did not like to see people waiting." As the door opened, flocks of people rushed in. They wanted to be first to grab their specialty bread or proscuitto or sfogliatelle. Some even bragged if they were first to get their chosen item.

One customer named Carl learned how to purchase his favorite rolls despite holiday crowds. Carl was new to the area and had discovered his favorite roll, ciabatta, in the Carlino's bread department. Carl didn't know the ways of the store around holiday time and he had not ordered ahead. He arrived before the store was open and the line had started. He didn't mind waiting but when the doors opened the store filled with new lines. He wandered around until he noticed half hidden, a small basket of his prized rolls. He quickly caught the attention of a staff person and said, "Are those ciabatta?" She answered yes they are. He said, "I'll take all of them!" With a bounce in his step, he happily left with a bag full of his favorites.

The local streets surrounding Carlino's suffer a drastic change when the holidays roll around. It's like a war unfolding in the streets. Police blow whistles and direct traffic in an attempt to control the chaos. SUVs and station wagons jockey for parking spots on the narrow street. Eager customers continue to stream in for hours to pick up their orders. God forbid, a storm is predicted. Apparently many locals live by the adage, "If you have to be stuck in the house, get Carlino's!"

"From Thanksgiving to January 1 it's mayhem!" exclaims Nick in his oh-my-God voice. "We just don't stop." He breaks into a sweat just talking about it. Then he rolls his eyes and an enigmatic smile comes out like sunshine after a shower. "But I love the fast pace!" The chefs suddenly look headachy and tired. One said, "It's the toughest part of the job." Some of Mama's holiday specialty items are extremely labor intensive, like the old-fashioned dish, Calcinetti. And, sadly for some customers, items often sell out. Fortunately custom-made baskets are always available and are popular choices as gifts. They often contain Carlino brand-name items such as special blend mustards, salad dressings, and award-winning signature extra virgin olive oil. And one can always top it off with biscotti.

Baccalà Salad

(Cod Fish Salad) *This dish is traditionally eaten on Christmas Eve.*

Serves: 4 | Time: Prep time is 30 minutes
(plus soaking time for the baccalà)

Cook time is 15 minutes.

PREPARATION OF SALT COD (BACCALÀ)

1. Rinse off the salt and let soak in cold water for 72 hours, changing the water 2-3 times daily.

2. After soaking, rinse baccalà and drain it well.

3. Then cut the baccalà into approximately 2 inch pieces and pick out any bones. Now it is ready for use!

INGREDIENTS:

1 pound salt cod, soaked, drained and cut
  (see preparation of Salt Cod above)
2 cloves garlic, chopped
4 tablespoons Extra Virgin Olive Oil
1 lemon, juiced
½ cup whole cured black olives

1 celery stalk, diced
½ teaspoon black pepper, freshly ground
¼ teaspoon red pepper flakes
1 sprig fresh Italian flat leaf parsley,
  chopped

DIRECTIONS:

1. In a heavy-bottomed skillet fry the baccalà pieces in ¼ cup olive oil until golden brown.

2. Remove baccalà with a slotted spoon. Place onto a paper-towel lined plate and continue to fry until all pieces are cooked.

3. When baccalà has completely cooled; place in a large mixing bowl add garlic, olives, celery, black pepper, red pepper, lemon juice, and olive oil.

4. Toss the baccalà with the garlic-olive mixture being careful not to break up the delicate fish.

5. Sprinkle in the chopped parsley.

6. Let sit at room temperature for 15-20 minutes before serving to insure the baccalà absorbs all the flavors.

ORECCHIETTE CON BROCCOLI DI RAPE E SALSICCIA

(Ear-shaped Pasta with Broccoli Rabe and Sausage)

Serves: 6 | Time: 35 minutes

INGREDIENTS:

2 pounds broccoli rabe, florets and tender stems only
¾ pound sweet Italian sausage, removed from casing
⅓ cup Extra Virgin Olive Oil
4 garlic cloves, crushed
1 tablespoon unsalted butter
1 cup chicken broth (use chicken stock if you have it available), plus more if
   necessary
⅓ cup Pecorino Romano cheese (preferably Locatelli)

DIRECTIONS:

1. In a large skillet, heat 1 tablespoon olive oil over medium heat. Add sausage meat and cook, breaking up the meat with a wooden spoon, for about 3-4 minutes or until no longer pink.

2. Add crushed garlic and red pepper flakes and continue cooking until the sausage is lightly browned, about 2 minutes longer.

3. In the meantime, bring a large pot of salted water to a boil.

4. Drain the fat from the skillet and add the remaining olive oil to the skillet.

5. Add ⅓ of the broccoli rabe to the pan and toss until it begins to wilt. Continue until all of the rabe is added and cover pan. Cook until all the rabe begins to wilt and turns a bright green color, about 5 minutes. Season with salt to taste. Add butter and stir to coat.

6. Add the chicken broth or stock and bring to a boil.

7. Reduce heat and simmer until the broccoli rabe become tender, about 15 minutes. If liquid begins to dissipate add additional stock ¼ cup at a time.

8. Bring 6 quarts water to a boil in a large pot. Add 2 tablespoons kosher salt.

9. Add orecchiette pasta and cook until al dente. Drain, reserving some of the pasta water, and return pasta to the pot. Reduce heat to medium low.

10. Add broccoli rabe and sausage mixture to the pasta pot. Add ½ of the grated Pecorino Romano cheese. Cook, stirring, for 1-2 minutes.

11. Transfer to a serving bowl and add the remaining grated cheese to top off the dish. Serve immediately.

Orecchiette con Broccoli di Rape e Salsiccia

Zuppa di Baccalà

(Cod Stew)

⤚ Serves: 3-4 | Prep time: 20 minutes ⤙
(plus 36-hour soaking time for the baccalà)

Cook time: 25 minutes

INGREDIENTS:

1 small onion, chopped
2 tablespoons Extra Virgin Olive Oil
¾ cup thinly sliced celery
Hot red pepper flakes
2 large potatoes, peeled, halved, and sliced into ½-inch pieces
1 pound baccala` (salted cod), soaked for at least 36 hours
4 fresh plum tomatoes, peeled, seeded and chopped, or canned tomatoes, chopped
1 to 2 teaspoons salt-preserved capers; rinsed well
8 to 10 black or green olives, pitted
1 sprig of rosemary, leaves only, discard stem
1 loaf crusty Italian bread, optional

DIRECTIONS:

1. In a large deep skillet, combine the onion and olive oil. Cook over medium heat until the onion is translucent being mindful not to brown. Stir in the celery and add a sprinkle of red pepper flakes. Cook, stirring for a minute or two.

2. Add the potatoes, and then add water to the halfway point (about ½ cup). Cover and cook, stirring occasionally, until the potatoes are barely tender, about 10 minutes.

3. Meanwhile, cut the baccalà into large chunks.

4. Add baccalà to the saucepan along with the tomatoes, capers, olives and rosemary.

5. Cook with the cover half closed until the baccalà is heated through, about 10 minutes.

6. Taste the sauce and add more pepper flakes if needed.

7. Serve the stew in shallow soup bowls with plenty of crusty bread for dipping!

Roasted Easter Lamb with White Wine

≈ Serves: 4 | Time: 3 hours ≈

INGREDIENTS:

2 to 2 ½ pounds spring lamb,
  preferably the shoulder
2 tablespoons vegetable oil
1 tablespoon butter
3 whole garlic cloves, peeled

1 sprig of fresh rosemary, leaves,
  chopped, or ½ teaspoon dried
  rosemary leaves
Salt and freshly ground black pepper
⅔ cup dry white wine

DIRECTIONS:

1. Wash the lamb thoroughly under cold running water and pat dry with cloth or paper towels.

2. Add the oil and butter in a large cast-iron pot, turn the heat on to medium high, and when the butter foam begins to subside, add in the lamb, the garlic, and the rosemary.

3. Brown the meat deeply all over, particularly the skin side. Check the garlic. If you find it is becoming very dark, remove it from the bottom of the pan and place it on top of the lamb.

4. Add salt, pepper to taste and the wine. Let the wine simmer briskly for about 20 seconds, turning the meat once or twice, then adjust heat to cook at a gently simmer and cover the pot, setting the lid on slightly ajar (half closed).

5. Cook for about 1 ½ to 2 hours, until the lamb is cooked all the way through and begins to come off the bone.

6. Turn the meat from time to time while it is cooking and, if the liquid in the pot has become insufficient; replenish it as often as needed with 2 to 3 tablespoons of water.

7. When done, transfer the lamb to serving platter. Tip the pan to spoon off all but a small amount of fat. Add 2 tablespoons of water, raise the heat to high, and while the water boils away use a wooden spoon to scrape loose cooking residues from the bottom and sides.

8. Pour the pot juices over the lamb.

9. Let rest for 10-15 minutes before serving to allow juices to distribute evenly throughout the meat.

Cicerchiata

(Honey Balls)

∾ Yield: 8 servings | Time: 1 hour ∾

INGREDIENTS:

3 cups all-purpose flour
4 eggs, beaten
¼ cup butter
½ cup sugar
½ teaspoon salt
2 teaspoons baking powder

1 tablespoon lemon zest
1 ½ cups honey
¾ cup pine nuts, or any other roasted,
chopped nuts
Colored nonpareils, for decoration

DIRECTIONS:

1. Melt the butter and set aside.

2. Mix 2 ½ cups of flour, sugar, baking powder, lemon zest, and salt in a large
   mixing bowl.

3. Make a well in the center of the flour mixture and carefully add the eggs and the
   melted butter into the well. Mix with a wooden spoon until just combined.

4. Complete mixing process with wooden spoon until dough pulls away from the
   sides of the bowl.

5. Using your hands, work in the remaining ½ cup of flour as needed.

6. Turn the dough out onto a lightly floured table. Knead dough until it is no
   longer sticky.

7. Break off small portions of the dough and roll into long thin strips. Cut dough
   into ⅛ inch bits using a knife or a pastry scraper.

8. Roll each bit pea-sized balls and set aside.

9. Fill a heavy-bottomed pot with 2 inches of oil. When hot, fry balls in small
   batches until golden brown color. Drain the balls on paper towels and set aside.

10. Bring 1 ½ cups of honey to a boil in a separate heavy-bottom pan. Boil the
    honey gently for 1-2 minutes and then add the fried dough balls. Stir with a
    wooden spoon until balls are well coated.

11. Remove balls from honey with a slotted spoon. Mound all of the honey balls on a large serving platter or in small clusters in paper baking cups.

   Mama would present the honey balls in two ways depending on the occasion. She would mound all of the honey balls into a large ring on her most decorative platter for the Christmas morning table.

   To make the ring shape: coat the outside of a standard drinking glass with cooking spray and place in the middle of the platter. Mound the honey balls around the glass to form a wreath shape. This makes for a great host or hostess gift. It is meant to be cut like a cake.

   Mama would mound the honey balls into individual decorative paper baking cups for other special occasions such as weddings, bridal or baby showers and communions. She would mound the honey balls into a pyramid shape in each cup. This method works great for special gatherings so that each guest can enjoy his or her very own treat.

12. Sprinkle surface evenly with nuts and/or nonpareils.

BOMBOLONI

(Italian-style Doughnuts)

≈ Yields: 12 | Time: 30 minutes ≈

INGREDIENTS:

1 cup all purpose flour
1 cup water mixed with 1 beaten egg
1 ½ cups shortening
1 ½ tablespoons active yeast

1 ½ teaspoons salt
Granulated sugar, for sprinkling
Crema Pasticcera *(recipe on page 149)*

DIRECTIONS:

1. Place sugar on a plate and set aside for later.

2. Place all ingredients into a large mixing bowl. Mix together for approximately 10 minutes.

3. Let the dough rest for roughly 5 minutes.

4. Turn dough out onto a floured surface.

5. Stretch the dough and fold it into 3 parts. Repeat this step two more times.

6. Place dough back into a bowl covered with plastic wrap and set in a warm place.

7. Once the dough has risen, roll out the dough to ½ inch thickness and cut out rounds with a 1 ½ inch diameter cutter.

8. Heat the oil in a deep fryer or heavy-bottomed pan until it reaches 350° F or 180° C.

9. Deep fry, without crowding the pan, turning each disc once or twice for even browning, until puffed and golden.

10. Drain the doughnuts on paper towel-lined pan.

11. Roll the hot doughnut in the sugar.

12. Serve the warm doughnuts with Crema Pasticcera on the side (to dip), or fill a pastry bag with the crema and fill the doughnuts.

Bomboloni

Pizza Rustica

(Italian Easter Meat Pie)

❧ Number of Servings: 6-8 | Time: 6-7 hours ❧

INGREDIENTS:

CRUST

5 ½ cups flour
¼ pound butter
2 teaspoons baking powder
2 eggs, well beaten
1 ½ teaspoons salt
1 ¼ cup warm water

FILLING

1 pepperoni, sliced thin
15 hard-boiled eggs, sliced
¼ pound piece salami cut in strips
¼ pound piece provolone, diced
¼ pound prosciutto, crumbled
1 small basket cheese, cubed

DIRECTIONS:

1. To prepare dough, blend the flour, baking powder and salt in a large bowl. Work in the butter with a fork until the flour resembles coarse meal.

2. Stir in the eggs and water gradually with a fork.

3. When just mixed, cover dough with wrap and refrigerate for 4 hours.

4. Bring dough to room temperature and divide dough in half. On a lightly floured board, roll out half the dough to ⅛ inch thickness and 14 inches around.

5. Place dough in a greased 12-inch pie plate.

6. Add the filling in the layers as follows: 5 sliced eggs, provolone, salami, 5 sliced eggs, basket cheese, pepperoni, prosciutto, 5 sliced eggs.

7. Roll out the remaining dough and cover pie.

8. Seal around with a fork. Use a knife or scissors to cut off excess.

9. Glaze top of dough with egg yolk and prick a few holes on top. Bake at 350° F for 50 minutes or until golden brown.

Serve slightly chilled and cut into wedges.

Zia Filomena's Orange Juice Cookies

*Mama's sister-in-law, Filomena, would make these delicious cookies for every family gathering. Aunt Phil's cookies are now a favorite of every generation of the Carlino clan!

❧ Yields: Approximately 30 cookies | Time: 45 minutes ❧

INGREDIENTS:

4 large eggs
1 ½ cups granulated sugar
4 teaspoons baking powder
1 cup freshly-squeezed orange juice

1 cup vegetable shortening
5 cups all-purpose flour
Powdered sugar, for dusting

DIRECTIONS:

1. Preheat oven to 350°F.

2. Beat the eggs and sugar on high with an electric or handheld mixer until they are smooth.

3. Lower speed to medium and slowly add the flour, orange juice, shortening, and baking powder until combined.

4. Pour mixture into a greased baking sheet.

5. Bake for 20 minutes or until golden brown.

6. Remove from oven and let cool for 15 minutes.

7. Cut cookies into 3-inch wide round shape using a cookie cutter.

8. Using a sifter dust powdered sugar on top of each cookie.

Zia Filomena and Zio Amedeo Carlino

Mama's Signature Calginetti

Chapter Thirteen
A Love of Pastry

Mama's talent as an innovative cook was a given, but her favorite activity in the kitchen, according to grandson Nick, was baking. "Mama was never trained professionally, but her love of creating made her an artist. With all her experience in making pasta, it was natural for her to expand her repertoire in baking."

By experimenting and applying what she learned, Mama created a set of keys to her signature creations. When it was time to pass the keys on to others, a little friction was created. Pastry Chef Jessica Perez worked beside Mama Carlino for more than seven years. In the early days a clash in viewpoint made for a difficult relationship. "I came from a corporate setting with my own vision," Jessica explains. "Working with Mama challenged me and I didn't always understand her words. She'd stand next to me and offer hints, lots of hints. My first impression of Mama was of the grandmother who liked to bake cookies all day. I wasn't interested in baking cookies, especially biscotti, which at that time I thought were boring. My impression was soon proven wrong as I developed a great respect for this grandmother whom I was soon to call chef."

"As we worked together sharing the same pastry table, I learned to listen carefully to her tone of voice. Depending on her tone I knew if it was thumbs up or down. I remember her strong hands from years of working the dough. Though I was skeptical at first I slowly began to embrace her techniques. Mama carried around a small blue book with her, which looked like an old-fashioned calendar date-book."

Nick moves toward a nearby closet and disappears for a few moments, "Ah, found it!" he says unearthing a small book from one of Mama's bags. Nick holds it out as if it is a Roman antiquity. Many recipes are scribbled or taped in the book, all smudged with cookie dough.

Jessica continues, "She never let this book leave her person. One day I said to her 'it's like your Bible.' From that day on we all called it Mama's Bible. As she taught me her recipes, she encouraged me to record them in a little book and now my book looks like hers."

Jessica's voice softens, "It seems like just yesterday I'd hear Mama say 'I feel lika I want to maka something today.' When Mama said 'I need 60 eggs,' I knew we were about to make a BIG batch. Mama did not measure; she didn't need to. I learned how much Mama used by counting what was left over after she was finished making a recipe. This is how we came to record the recipes."

An important lesson for Jessica came when she could not locate her missing timer. "As I scouted the area looking for it, Mama asked, 'wadda you need this?' I retorted that baking without a timer is like baking without an oven! She said in a low gruff-growl, 'You pay atten!' and then she popped biscotti in the oven and moved on, while I was responsible for rotating every pan, feeding the ovens, and trying to find enough cooling racks to accommodate all her cookies. She taught me to pay attention to everything around me, not just a buzzer."

Jessica also learned that cooking the old-world way meant rules could be broken. She explains with a look of amusement, "One day I observed Mama putting a big pot of chocolate and water on the burner. She directed me by saying, 'Put on the stoov and stir.' I couldn't believe she would mix chocolate and water together. That combination is forbidden in the pastry chef world. I argued to no end. I kept telling her you don't add water to chocolate, it wouldn't work. 'You stir,' Mama repeated.

"The outcome was unbelievable. With constant stirring the mixture changed into a very soft texture which was almost cake-like after it was baked. Since then I have used this method countless times. It is one of the secrets to a filling we use in our fruit-filled biscotti and our calginetti filling."

One of Chef Jessica's favorite recipes is Italian peaches. Typically, this pastry was only made for special occasions, such as weddings. Jessica used to beg Mama to let her make them to sell in the store. Mama's answer was always the same, 'Not until my Angela gets married, then we sell.'" Jessica now makes them for the store and proudly states, "Whenever I see how beautiful they look and I receive compliments from customers, I think of Mama's words and smile. I know how proud she must be."

The smell of cinnamon and sugar rises as a tray of what Jessica calls "scraps" is pulled out of the oven and placed on a rack. "Another important lesson was that Mama never, ever threw out anything," Jessica says with emphasis. "Scraps are a good example. Left over pie dough is pinched into small shapes, sprinkled with cinnamon and sugar, and baked till crunchy. Jessica dips the little morsels warm from the oven in powdered sugar. The taste and crunch is magnificent; they melt in your mouth! Today employees are in for a treat!"

Jessica packages up the scraps and will send them out with the next delivery to the other Carlino store. Shipments of prepared foods are trucked over several times a day and this day Jessica honors Mama's tradition of giving the staff a surprise.

A warm culture is evident in the Carlino kitchen. The kitchen was and still is the central meeting place. As Jessica pours cream into a pot of steaming liquid, she says to Megan, her assistant, "Employees, family, and friends all come to the kitchen. They might ask 'you got anything for me?' with a look of hope. Yeah, they die for brownie scraps! But it's also the place to come if they want to talk about a secret."

All of Mama's recipes are made according to her methods. "All our chefs are trained to make recipes exactly the way she liked," Jessica said. "We will continue to honor these traditions and cook from our hearts."

It is time for Jessica to put the finishing touches on a cake. She carefully arranges the famous biscotti cookies on top of a beautiful three-layer dark-chocolate cake. Her job is demanding, the pressure is on to keep up with the orders, but she stands aside for a moment, pointing to a photo of herself with Mama. The two are close together decorating a strawberry shortcake. A look of accomplishment illuminates their faces.

Jessica's eyes stay focused on the photo as her voice clouds, "Every day when I take my place at the pastry table I stand alone; no one works in the space where Mama used to stand. I am still sharing the table with Mama . . . and I always will. I'm holding her space."

CREMA PASTICCERA

(Italian Pastry Cream)

"Mama's Italian Pastry Crema was another one of those core recipes she used for many things. Mama placed the crema in the center of the Italian Wedding Peaches. She also used this crema for cream puffs (Mama especially liked to make her cream puffs into the shape of a swan). She also used this crema as the filling for her Bomboloni and Italian Rum Cakes."

- Chef Jessica

*Crema Pasticcera is not difficult to make at all. It does; however, require care because when left unattended the eggs could curdle very quickly.

**The crema should be transferred to a bowl as soon as it's ready, because it will continue to cook in the pot, making the crema too thick, and, again, cooking the eggs to curdle

⤜ Time: 25 minutes ⤛

INGREDIENTS:

6 tablespoons flour	the yolks of 6 fresh eggs
¾ cup sugar	2 cups whole milk
1 vanilla bean	A pinch of salt

DIRECTIONS:

1. Bring 1 ½ cups of milk to warm temperature. Scrape the vanilla bean and add to pot along with the vanilla bean pod.

2. Lightly whisk the eggs in a medium size mixing bowl along with the flour and sugar making sure no lumps form.

3. Add the remaining ½ cup of milk to make a paste-like consistency.

    By this time the milk on the stove will be about ready to boil.

4. Strain the milk into the egg/flour mixture. Return the cream to the pot and put back on the stovetop over low heat, stirring gently, until it barely reaches a slow boil.

5. Once the cream thickens a bit and boils lightly it is done.

6. Transfer the cream to a bowl and let cool. Place a piece of plastic directly on top of the cream to prevent a skin from forming across the top.

CHAPTER 14
MAMA'S BLESSINGS

On a weekday morning with the customary sounds of coffee perking and the morning news anchor announcing the headlines of the day, Pat and Mama sit in the family room enjoying their morning routine. Pat sips his coffee sleepily and Mama is dressed for work. Pat discusses the new start-up store in West Chester. "I'm just not sure how things are going to pan out," he said. "It's a large endeavor."

Mama notes the concern in his voice, smiles reassuringly, and reaches over and gives him a kiss on the cheek. Then she says, "I have no doubts, everything is going to work out great. Don't worry. It's going to be a success." She then closes her eyes in contentment.

A few nights earlier while her family put the final polish on the retail area of the brand new store, she had made a secret pilgrimage to the lower level to add her own touches. Unbeknownst to her family, she took the steps to the lower level with hammer in hand and in her formidable fashion she banged a nail in the wall. Then she lifted a framed picture of Padre Pio and hung it perfectly on the wall. Taking a moment to gaze at him eye-to-eye, she whispers, "Va bene." Then she turns as she hears footsteps coming down the stairs. Smiling a warm welcome to the family priest she says "grazie" as he holds his hands in a blessing and commences to bless the new market. Mama has instilled her faith, now she can rest.

Pat places his coffee cup on the table and continues watching the news. He asks Mama a question but she does not answer. He looks over and is stunned. Her head is leaning back, her eyes are staring, and she is moaning. Pat grabs her arm, frantically yelling, "Mama what's wrong? What's wrong?" Then he yells for Laura who is upstairs. Mama is not responding. In heart-pounding panic Pat yells again, "Laura something is wrong with Mama!"

Laura rushes down the stairs, takes one look at Mama, and calls 911. The children, hurrying for school, lunge down the stairs and chaos erupts. Laura instructs Angela to take the children back upstairs. After four long minutes Laura calls 911 again in desperation. A siren blares in the street and seconds later an ambulance screeches into the driveway. EMTs maneuver Mama onto a stretcher and quickly transport her and Pat to the local hospital. Laura follows in her car.

Tests are ordered. Suspecting a stroke, Pat calls his friend John DiMichele who joins him for an overnight stay by her side.

In the morning a neurologist explains to the family a drug can be given but it is not likely to reverse the massive hemorrhage in her brain. The drug is given but has no effect. Mama's right side is paralyzed. Laura feels it is essential to pick up the children and bring them to be with Mama. Late in the afternoon the family gathers in Mama's room. Nick sits close to Mama's head while Nadia lies on Mama's chest. Nick's head is pounding with confusion and worry. He decides to speak and leans close to Mama, "Mi sono perso," he says. I am lost. There is movement under the sheet covering as Mama frees her hand and reaches toward him. She somehow manages to button his sweater. The effort exhausts her and her hand drops.

The doctors are not sure how much control she has of her arms. After 24 hours the test results are disheartening. Her condition has worsened. She is breathing with the help of a respirator. Philip sits close to the railing of the bed and tries valiantly not to cry. Mama is aware of his presence. She reaches her hand toward Philip, who is wearing his school uniform, finds his collar, and turns it up. The gesture indicates that she loves him. Angela; Mama's namesake is numb with grief. Joe; Angela's boyfriend of just a few months is experiencing this tremendous loss with Angela, and he would later tell her that at that point he knew he wanted to spend the rest of his life with her.

After a brutally long sleepless night the neurologist convenes a meeting with Nicola, Pat, Laura, and Uncle Frank and relays in a monotone voice, "She will not recover."

Pat stoically walks the hospital halls down to Mama's room. Coming close he puts his arms around her. He feels the coolness of her skin and whispers, "You can not leave us Mama, the children need you." There is a rustle of the sheet as Mama turns her head away from him. One tear slowly falls down her cheek and with her functioning arm she pushes Pat away. This is the last time she moves.

Pat knew in that moment he had to let his mother go. She was telling him she did not want to be a burden, it was her time to rest in peace.

Weeping, Pat returns to the family waiting outside.

Chapter Fifteen

Graduation

Rap music thumps to a consistent beat and laughter echoes through the trees as guests pass through the black iron gate and take in the scene. Nick's graduation pool-party is spooling up, ready to take off.

Angela, Pat, Laura, and Nick are all busily attending to newcomers, welcoming them with hugs and a choice of drinks. Friends and relatives gather to share in a joyous event, Mama's first grandchild graduating from college. Her beloved Nicky completed his program at Saint Josephs' University and his diploma is displayed on a decorated table along with his cap and gown for all to admire. Red and yellow blossoms float enticingly on the surface of the backyard pool as children edge into the cool water. Flowers bloom bright red in gracious pots and a figure of a fairy sits in quiet corner contemplating the happy crowd.

In a Phillies hat and shorts Pat cranks up the heat on two over-sized grills filled with flank steak, chicken legs, and mini-hamburgers. Shrimp on skewers lie marinating in a colorful dish. Laura arranges tray after tray of antipasto, gooey brie-like cheeses, and a fig spread sweet and delicious. Each dish is exquisitely laid out on a beautifully draped stage in the sunroom.

Mama might have made the rectangle-shaped pizzelle filled with pastry cream. Rosanna places her famous creamy cheesecake on the table. Chef Jessica made the honorary graduation cake called Tropix, a vanilla bean cake soaked in pina colada syrup, filled with guava cream. The frosting for this yum of a cake is a butter cream with toasted shaved coconut. Highlighting the top of the cake is a perfectly formed black academic cap made of fondant.

On this 90-degree spring day of celebration Nick wears Bermuda shorts and sports a freshly gelled short haircut. He's full of laughter as he jokes with his college friends, enjoying icy cold cocktails under a canopy by the pool, while his brother Philip shepherds his younger cousins. They scurry in and around the patio and pool, dipping in and out, hanging on to the edge, and skipping through a myriad of adults. Philip is watching and his eyes seem to say, "Be safe."

With a gentle touch on the shoulder and a shy smile, Philip guides his young friend Giovanni, John and Kathy's son. The boy needs to wear headgear for protection due to severe hemophilia and autism. Philip's gestures are that of a deeply caring person with a layer of wisdom lying close to the surface. Like a young bird posted on a rooftop surveying the world before him, he sees many options ahead. Perhaps Mama's clear goal-setting ways have patterned him; for sure, his nurturing side will take him far.

Nadia ribs him in a loud teasing tone, "You are a hermit!" What that means is Philip can often be found in the big overstuffed armchair in the family room watching the Phillies battle. Like his father, he adores baseball and wears Philly-fan-appropriate dress: a baseball cap, shorts, and red and white T-shirt. Looking toward his future, he gives voice with his thoughtful nature, "I might combine writing with my passion for sports or maybe I'll become a vet or doctor." It's a different focus but his sensitivity is compelling. Mama would be so pleased to see this young man's orientation toward doing good work.

Angela, eye catching in a bright sundress, sits close beside her husband Joe Milani as he reminisces. "In the short time I knew Mama one thing was clear to me, Angela and she ran on parallel tracks; both are artistic, full of love, and of the same mind!" He glances over at Angela with a thoughtful look and says, "Yeah, I know why they call her Mama Carlino Junior!"

As the day's rays bend into semi-darkness, little white twinkle lights flicker strategically around the pool. Many have left to tuck their youngsters into bed and the mood has mellowed. The D.J. is packing up the sound system and lights. Nicola, leaning on his cane, ambles along the side yard watering 18 young tomato plants perfectly spaced from each other in a raised brick bed. Perhaps they remind him of Mama, the woman of the earth, storing up and ready to burst forth with giving.

Pat sits in the long shadows reflecting, comfortable in a cushioned deck chair. It's been another long day of preparation and cooking; he is watching and thinking. Memories flutter within him as a few brave insects come out to the night.

Softly he says, "People often ask me if I'm upset or angry at losing Mama so soon." Casting his dark eyes out, he rests his chin in his hand and in a philosophical tone says, "Her goal was to create a better way of life for her family. I have no regrets. She fulfilled the first part of her life by raising two sons; she was able to work out of her home. In the second part of her life she started a business with her children. She wanted to leave a legacy for her kids and grandkids to enjoy! She accomplished this. I have no regrets."

Laura emerges from the shadows. She still has a bit of pep in her step despite dancing and entertaining for hours. She touches her husband's back and says, "Come on, we need to load up the van and return dishes and platters to the store." Then she jokes, "I'm not going to work tomorrow!" Pat rises from his chair and they walk off together into darkness toward the next destination.

Chapter 16

Intuitions

All of Mama's closest family and friends were well aware of her intrinsic and targeted intuition.

Alejandro Perez, the sturdily built, talented executive chef who works at the Carlino's Ardmore store has his fair share of anecdotes. As he slices through a flank steak, which peels away like butter, his face draws tight with emotion as he recalls an incident occurring just three days before Mama passed away. Pausing in his work, he takes a breath and in a reflective tone says, "Mama and I were working hard cooking for the opening at the West Chester store. I was feeling worried about getting everything done in time. Suddenly Mama said, 'Alejandro, you need espresso now!' Mama brought me upstairs to the private kitchen and motioned me to sit down. 'Eat,' she said placing biscotti before me. As the room filled with the familiar smell of espresso beans, Mama said in a between-you-and-me tone, 'I tell you things now because soon I'll be in Conshohocken.'" (The Carlino burial ground is located in Conshohocken.)

Alejandro was worried by the tone in Mama's voice. "What's going on, Mama?" he asked. "'I want to be at rest,' Mama said simply. I said, 'Mama, no! It's not your time.' But Mama had stated her feelings and that was the end of it."

When she passed away three days later, Alejandro shared this story with his wife. In time they took comfort telling each other, "Some things you do not understand but we know she loved us and that's all we know."

Another poignant episode happened with a coffee connection.

The family built the business cookie-by-cookie, pasta-by-pasta, soup-by-soup. All are made from the heart with family members relying on one another, sharing decisions, and growing. It was incomprehensible that Mama was no longer the center of the family's orbit. But like a dream, family members experienced her presence in sundry ways.

The day after her passing Pat and Laura woke as a new day etched slivers of light onto their bedroom wall. Laura recalls it clearly, "I woke up and immediately looked over at Pat. I saw he had tears in his eyes. After a moment his expression changed, he seemed mystified and he asked me, 'Do you hear that?' I heard nothing, but he continued, 'I hear her pouring water in the coffee maker.' After a few minutes passed we both smelled an incredible familiar coffee aroma coming up the stairs and I looked at Pat in disbelief, 'Do you smell that?' He nodded and we just stared at each other in amazement. Mama was there making coffee like she always does! Her spirit in an ethereal way was still with us."

Mama had always pushed the edges of life, her love coming through as strong and upright as the special strain of tomatoes the family grew in the back yard. With eyes heavy with memories, Laura softens and says in a small voice, "We are both grateful."

Grandson Nick also states his gratitude in a story about his time with Mama in her last days. During those hectic days before the opening of the second store, Nick chauffeured Mama between the two stores. Nick recalls fondly, "Mama's favorite ice cream was at Friendly's. She'd say to me, grinning, 'I won't eat all day but I want my ice cream. It's my guilty pleasure!'" En route to West Chester Nick spontaneously pulled off the highway into Mama's favored ice cream establishment. Settled in the familiar red upholstered booth, Mama ordered vanilla ice cream with the brittle chocolate cap on top. Sitting across from one another, licking their yummy ice-cold treats, they laughed like two kids skipping school.

Nick feels lucky to have had this private interlude of joy and sharing with Mama. Perhaps he has inherited some of her intuition as well.

Panna Cotta

(Italian Cooked Cream)

~ Yield: 6 | Time: 35 minutes ~

INGREDIENTS:

1 package (¼ ounce) unflavored
  powdered gelatin
½ cup cold milk
2 ½ cups heavy cream
½ cup confectioners' sugar

½ fresh vanilla bean, scraped
Zest of ¼ small orange

6 small (4-6 ounce) ramekins

DIRECTIONS:

1. Sprinkle the gelatin over the cold milk in a small bowl and let sit for 15-20 minutes. The gelatin will absorb the milk and become "spongy".

2. Combine the cream, vanilla bean scrapings and the pod, orange zest, and confectioners' sugar in a medium saucepan and bring to a slight simmer.

3. Stir to dissolve sugar. Set aside to let the vanilla bean steep.

4. Remove from heat and strain.

5. Return mixture to a clean pan, and stir in the gelatin mixture.   Continue stirring on low heat until the gelatin has completely dissolved (you should not see any gelatin particles).

6. Pour the prepared cream into the ramekins.

7. Place the ramekins in the refrigerator to chill for at least four hours or overnight.

Panna Cotta

Mama's granddaughter,
Chef Angela

Chapter Seventeen

Future Visions

Chef Angela heeds her grandmother's words: "Work from the heart, not just from the hands; it comes from inside!"

Beaming in her bright pink jacket, she greets kids as they enter a Carlino's cooking class. The large sunny room is decorated in every shade of pink and accented with balloons, colorful tablecloths, and large jars of candy.

After thorough hand washing each young chef is outfitted in a white paper chef's hat and an apron. They take their places at a table set up with a cup of grapes, a box of popcorn, and a small bottle of water. They are small snacks for hungry tummies. Lively music plays in the background as assistants Nadia, Nick, and Gilda bring out trays of white pie-shaped mixture.

All eyes are on Chef Angela as she calls out in a bounding tone, "It looks like a white flat cake but it's actually a fluffy marshmallow mix. Now get your cutouts ready." She demonstrates by taking a star cutout and presses it into the gooey mixture while saying, "Press. Press." Then she instructs, "Sprinkle time!" Little cups filled with an assortment of colored sprinkles are laid on the table in front of each child. "Dip any color you want," adds the chef turned magician with a flourish of her hands. One little girl named Sophie can't resist tasting the sprinkle combo. As she licks her fingers, her eyes grow wide. Chef Angela laughs easily and says, "When the shapes are covered with sprinkles they aren't sticky any more."

The next course is cake pops. These fun little cakes, frozen to hold their shape, look like upside down lollipops.

Chef Angela demonstrates. "Do a little twirl," she sings as she swirls the pop in pink melted chocolate. The room fills with sweet aromas: vanilla, cake, and chocolate. One little girl with long wavy hair says, "I have chocolate in my hair." Chef Angela responds, "So do I! Good thing it comes out."

For a final artistic treat she announces, "The art of drizzling." It's a Pollock painting in the making. Popcorn is spread out on flat trays. Angela tips giant stainless steel pots

Angela and Nadia

filled with four colors of melted chocolate, drizzling the top of the flat popcorn cake. In a frenzy of artistic abandon the children add their own drizzles, splatters, and blobs accompanied with squeals of laughter. Like Mama, Chef Angela is dreaming of bigger audiences.

Angela, Nick and Mama at the opening of the West Chester store- 2007

All four of the Carlino girls- 2005

Chocolate Candy Covered Bananas

"As I always say, 'be creative when making your recipes!' Be sure to dip your chocolate covered bananas into your favorite toppings. Have fun and enjoy your treat!" Chef Angela

CHEF ANGELA'S RECIPE

Yields: 6 chocolate covered bananas | Time: 20 minutes, plus freezing time

INGREDIENTS:

3 whole bananas
1 cup semi-sweet chocolate chips
2 tablespoons heavy cream

Your favorite toppings (Chef Angela likes granola, walnut pieces, peanut butter chips, butterscotch chips or graham cracker crumbs)

DIRECTIONS:

1. Cut bananas in half crosswise so you have smaller looking bananas. Poke Popsicle sticks through the flat bottom of each piece of banana.

2. Place a piece of parchment paper on a cookie sheet and lay all the bananas on the pan. Place in freezer for 1 hour or more.

3. Meanwhile, set up your toppings bar. Add each different topping to a flat plate so that you can dip the banana (with chocolate) into the topping.

4. When the bananas have completely frozen ask your adult helper for help with the chocolate step. Carefully heat up the chocolate chips and the cream together in a saucepan over low heat and mix with a rubber spatula until the chips have completely melted.

5. Take the chocolate off of the hot stovetop. Dip one banana at a time into the chocolate sauce while holding the popsicle stick. While the chocolate is still melted dip the banana into your favorite topping. Lay the banana back onto the cookie sheet so the chocolate can harden.

6. When you finish decorating every banana place the cookie sheet back into the freezer for 6 hours or overnight to give them time to really become a yummy frozen treat!

Party Snack Mix

Be sure to be extra creative when making this recipe, and add some of your favorite snack foods. Remember to always add a dried fruit and a crunchy nut or granola before adding any type of candy or salty food to really make this a super snack! – Chef Angela

CHEF ANGELA'S RECIPE

INGREDIENTS:

1 cup craisins
½ cup raisins
1 cup unsalted almonds

1 ½ cups candy coated chocolate candies
3 cups whole wheat waffle pretzels
3 cups cheddar fish-shaped crackers

DIRECTIONS:

1. Carefully add all the ingredients into a large mixing bowl.

2. Use a spoon, or 2 very clean hands, because your hands are your best tools, to mix up all the ingredients.

3. Serve right in the bowl and share with your friends and family or ask an adult helper to help pour the snack mix into an airtight container for later snacking!

Easy Morning Muffins

"Substitute the blueberries for any other ingredient that you may like. For an added treat I like to make my muffins with chocolate chips and walnuts. Yum!" – Chef Angela

Yield 12 muffins | 12 = 1 dozen! | Time: 35 minutes

INGREDIENTS:

1 cup all-purpose flour
1 cup whole wheat flour
3 teaspoons baking powder
½ teaspoon salt
¾ cup white sugar

1 egg
1 cup milk
¼ cup vegetable oil
1 cup fresh blueberries

DIRECTIONS:

1. Ask your adult helper to preheat the oven to 400°F.

2. Stir together the flours, baking powder, salt and sugar in a large bowl.

3. In a smaller bowl carefully crack the egg into the bowl and whisk the milk and oil together with the egg.

4. Pour the egg mixture into the flour mixture.

5. Mix all of the ingredients together. Use a fork for this step!

6. Add the blueberries and mix lightly. Be sure not to mix too much. Now you have a batter! Congratulations!

7. Line a muffin pan with muffin papers and pour the batter in each paper. Be sure not to fill all the way to the top!

8. Bake for 20 minutes or until golden brown.

9. Enjoy!

Pizza Margherita

❧ Yield: 1 - 12" pizza | Time: 10 minutes ❧

INGREDIENTS:

1 prepared dough ball, *(recipe on page 37)*
¼ cup prepared pizza sauce
2 large fresh ovoline mozzarella balls (egg size) or 12 fresh ciliegine mozzarella balls
  (cherry size), drained and dried with a paper towel, sliced thinly

Classically this pizza is made with buffalo mozzarella. If you are unable to find buffalo mozzarella, cow's milk mozzarella will work just fine!

Extra Virgin Olive Oil, to drizzle
Sea salt and pepper, to taste
6-10 fresh basil leaves, cut into strips, or left whole

DIRECTIONS:

1. Set a pizza stone in the oven and preheat oven to 500°F. Allow the stone to heat in the hot oven for 45 minutes to 1 hour before cooking the pizza.

2. On a floured surface, stretch the pizza dough to about a 12 inch diameter.

3. Transfer the dough to a floured pizza peel.

4. Add the tomato sauce to the center of the dough, and using the bottom of a ladle, spread the sauce with a circular motion until you reach about 1 inch from the edge.

5. Place the mozzarella cheese evenly on the pizza.

6. Drizzle with olive oil and sprinkle sea salt and pepper to flavor the mozzarella.

7. Carefully place the prepared pizza on the pizza stone and cook until the bottom is charred, about 8-10 minutes.

8. Sprinkle or place the basil leaves on the pizza. Return to oven to cook for 2 minutes longer.

   This is the classic pizza margherita recipe. The Carlino family loves to make the fresh version of this recipe in the summer months when tomatoes are in season.

   Instead of adding the pizza sauce to the crust, drizzle olive oil and 1 garlic clove, chopped, sea salt and pepper, to taste. Place the pizza on the stone and cook for 8 minutes, or until the bottom is charred.

   Arrange the fresh mozzarella, 2 fresh tomatoes, sliced, and fresh basil on top of the cooked pizza crust and return to oven for 2 minutes longer.

Pizza Margherita

TIMELINE

1980 Mama cooks and bakes out of her home—the start of her famous biscotti. Homemade pasta is a winner, with sales increasing continually.

1983 The Carlinos rent a barbershop on the same street as their home. They renovate it into a retail space to sell products and Mama increases her output.

1984 Mama begins selling homemade pasta to the local farmers markets, including Downingtown. The farmers market in Wayne offers Mama's homemade goods.

1985 Bakers are brought over from Italy to teach rustic bread making techniques.

1986 The Carlinos purchase the building and expand the space by renovating an apartment located in the back. Pasta production is greatly enhanced.

1988 A twin house next door becomes available and is purchased. They need a bigger retail area to sell pastas, pastries, cold cuts, and cheeses and to expand the prepared dishes.

1992 They purchase a twin that is attached to the first twin. They close the driveway between the two and enlarge the retail area again. Pastry production also increases.

1999 Carlino's expands again and they move pastry production upstairs.

2004 Pat Carlino begins scouting for a suitable second location. They ask their customer base for input. West Chester is a growing city with retail establishments, a university, and a courthouse. Mama hears "young people are moving to Chester County." She has friends who live there and she particularly likes the bucolic farms in the area. She says, "The young are there so we need to be there."

2006 A store is purchased on Market Street. Plans begin for a much larger establishment with a café for customers to sit and enjoy a bite to eat. It is an enormous undertaking as they plan a huge underbelly where all the preparation would take place. Chef Louis helps in the organization. It takes a year to get the approvals to renovate the store.

2007 Grand opening of Carlino's in West Chester. Ironically Mama passed away on her 70th birthday, just a few days after the opening.

INDEX OF RECIPES